THE
PARTISANS

THE PARTISANS

David Mountfield

HAMLYN
London New York Sydney Toronto

Published by
The Hamlyn Publishing Group Limited
London · New York · Sydney · Toronto
Astronaut House, Feltham, Middlesex, England

Phototypeset in England by Keyspools Limited,
Golborne, Lancs.
Printed in England by Hazell Watson & Viney Limited,
Aylesbury, Bucks.

*Endpapers: A Russian detachment greet their beleaguered
comrades at Stalingrad.*

*Half-title: A woman member of the French Resistance in
Paris, 1944.*

Title page: A Russian partisan taken by the Germans.

Acknowledgements
Associated Press, London 162 top; Central Press Photos,
London 96 bottom, 109 bottom right; Czechoslovak News
Agency, Prague 6 bottom, 26, 30, 31 top left and right;
Hamlyn Group Picture Library, London 15, 41, 44, 52 top,
132; Imperial War Museum, London 82 top, 123 bottom;
Keystone Press Agency, London half-title, title, 12, 19 top,
24, 31 bottom, 36 top, 45 top, 66 top, 70, 76, 77 top right, 92,
96 top, 97, 100, 109 bottom left, 110 bottom, 111 top, 117 top,
122 bottom, 137 top right, 138 bottom, 139 top, 150, 162
bottom, 163, 182 bottom, 183; MacClancy Press, London
endpapers, 6 top, 45 centre and bottom, 52 bottom, 53, 60
bottom, 64, 65, 66 bottom, 87, 109 top, 111 bottom, 116 top,
117 bottom, 128, 137 top left, 137 bottom, 138 top, 139
bottom, 170, 176, 178 bottom, 182 top, 184; Mansell
Collection, London 18 top right; Popperfotos, London 18
bottom, 19 bottom, 156 top right; Private collections 18 top
left, 156 top left, 156 bottom, 157; Rijksinstituut voor
Oorlogsdocumentatie, Amsterdam 86 top left and right, 86
bottom; H. Roger-Viollet, Paris 110 top, 116 bottom, 123
top; Tanum-Norli, Oslo 60 top, 77 top left, 77 bottom; U.S.
Army Photograph 122 top.

Contents

Introduction   7

Albania   13

Czechoslovakia   25

Poland   37

Denmark   61

Norway   71

Netherlands   83

Belgium   93

France   101

Yugoslavia   129

Greece   151

Russia   171

Index   191

Above: Partisan activity was frequently most successful in disrupting the enemy's communications, as here in Russia.

Below: The partisans' life in the forests was often remote from the political decisions that determined the level of aid from the Allies.

Introduction

THIS BOOK is about militant resistance to the Axis in occupied countries of Europe during the Second World War. That is a very large and complex subject which can scarcely be summarised in a single volume, and it has been necessary to impose strict limits on the subject matter. Certain aspects have been excluded, sometimes on arbitrary though necessary grounds. For example, resistance to the regime in the Axis countries themselves is not discussed, and that includes the extensive Italian resistance to the Germans after September 1943 when Italy became a 'co belligerent' with the Allies. There is also little mention of the activities of Allied organizations such as the British SOE (Special Operations Executive) or the American OSS (Office of Strategic Services) except when they were intimately involved with developments in a particular country.

The word partisan in the sense of a guerrilla fighter dates from the early 18th century. It was used to describe the Russian guerrillas who harassed the French during Napoleon's retreat from Moscow, and in the popular mind today it is particularly associated with guerrilla groups in Eastern Europe, mostly Communist-inspired, fighting in mountains or forested regions against the Germans during the Second World War. The followers of Tito in Yugoslavia and the behind-the-lines units in the Soviet Union are indeed known simply as 'the Partisans', and it is those countries above all others that spring to mind when partisans are mentioned.

In this book, as implied in the first sentence on this page, a somewhat wider definition is adopted. Irregular warfare by substantial groups operating over a period of months or years was only possible in countries where geography permitted it. In a country like Denmark or the Netherlands the requisite conditions did not exist; but to exclude such countries from a general survey of this kind would be to make too sharp a distinction since militant resistance—sabotage, assassination, even armed raids—existed there also. On the other hand this book is not intended to be a record of 'resistance' in general, which includes many non-militant activities such as espionage or the organization of escape routes. The main concern is with more or less full-time guerrilla operations; but in countries where circumstances dictated that this type of resistance was minimal or non-existent, some account–inevitably brief–is attempted of the alternative activities in which militant resistance groups engaged.

Although this book is not about politics, it would be impossible to leave politics entirely out of account. The great majority of active resistance leaders were concerned with something more than the ejection of the occupying forces. They looked beyond the end of the war to the society that would exist when the Germans had gone. Some of them wished merely to restore the *status quo ante*. A larger and in general more effective number aimed to achieve a different type of society. Revolution, the Soviet Communist Party advised, would be achieved through liberation, and in many cases it would be hard to say which was the primary aim of the partisans–the defeat of the enemy or the acquisition of power. They were, perhaps, but two sides of the same coin. Thus it happened that in Greece and the Balkans particularly but in some other countries too, rival guerrilla organizations spent much of their effort fighting each other rather than fighting the Germans.

The Allies, on whose aid to a varying extent the partisans depended, customarily declared that they were only interested in who was doing the enemy the most damage, and they certainly made efforts to reconcile rival partisan groups in order to develop more potent resistance. Yet they too looked, or should have looked, beyond the final defeat of Germany, and in places where their claim to be politically disinterested was not demonstrably false (if indeed there were any such places), their neutrality was impractical. Resistance leaders knew that they were likely to be exploited by the major powers, and most of them were fairly adept at exploitation on their own account. The cynical bargaining of Churchill and Stalin at Yalta over post-war power zones in Europe, or the betrayal of a gallant ally like Abbas Kupi, could be matched by the duplicity of partisan leaders who disguised their real aims in order to secure external approbation or arms for the internal power struggle.

The aims of the Allies and the aims of the partisans rarely coincided. The Allies required either destruction of specific strategic targets or in some circumstances the tying-down of enemy troops to prevent their use on the fighting front. The British and the Americans were often wary of encouraging too potent a guerrilla force where undesirable political ends were in view and they were unwilling to encourage full-scale revolt in occupied countries which was likely to end in disaster. The attitude of the Soviet Union was, of course, different because Moscow hoped to extend its influence in Europe by Communist revolution. Communists were less inhibited by the fear of reprisals, and to them partisan warfare was a more honourable and more natural means of resistance than it had traditionally been regarded in the West. 'Mass risings, revolutionary methods and guerrillas everywhere are the means of re-establishing numerical and material equality,' Marx had said, and he had poured scorn on the idea that a country should cease to resist when its regular forces were defeated.

However, except in the Soviet Union itself (where the situation was different in that the partisans and the regular forces were fighting together with no other power involved), Moscow had a mixed record of support for resisters, and it sometimes turned out that there were as many differences between Moscow and Communist guerrillas in other countries as there were between such guerrillas and the western Allies. Tito started his movement as a loyal supporter of Moscow. By 1945 his position had changed somewhat. As he remarked, he had received more help from the British than the Russians, and in spite of his profound suspicion of British motives he got on much better with British liaison officers, who included a Conservative MP and an Oxford don, than he did with the rather unhelpful emissaries of Moscow. Indeed, Tito has always appeared, considering his political position, a surprisingly attractive figure to the West. In contrast with certain other guerrilla leaders of the Left, he was a statesman, not a savage.

All war is horrifying, and irregular warfare is perhaps the most beastly, most cruel form. Individual deeds of gallantry and humanity notwithstanding, in irregular warfare the most contemptible behaviour becomes normal, even commendable. The psychotic and the criminal become valuable members of society. Law, truth, justice, mean nothing. Atrocities, massacres on a hardly believable scale, torture, betrayal, falsehood, swindling, deadly hatred—horrors of every kind become part of everday life. It affects everyone: not only the guerrilla fighting desperately for survival, or the ordinary citizen caught between contending forces, but also those who, from safe office desks, plan the next move in the battle of dirty tricks. One tiny and insignificant example, a mere matter of office politics really, may suggest the moral atmosphere.

When Brigadier Fitzroy Maclean joined Tito's Partisans as the chief British liaison officer, his entry into Yugoslavia was organized by the appropriate organization, which at the time was SOE (Cairo). But Maclean was not an SOE man; he was a direct emissary of Churchill, and his appointment was resented by SOE (Cairo). When he arrived in Egypt, he was surprised to be confronted by total non-cooperation from the men who were supposed to brief him. Not only were the relevant files kept from him, he discovered that a whispering campaign was being secretly organized to put it about that he was 'not the man for the job', that he had a bad 'black spot' on his record, even that he was a sexual deviant. A deprecatory telegram was sent to London over the signature of the commander-in-chief, who would never have known about it but for the brusque response it provoked from Churchill. The campaign was checked, its organizer ordered into line, and in due course Maclean boarded an aeroplane to fly to Yugoslavia. But as he remarks in an off-hand way that nevertheless sends a chill down the spine, on the aircraft that was to drop him to the Partisans he was careful not to take the first parachute he was offered.

This is hardly the type of morality suggested by all those stories about gallant British agents.

It is easier to cite that small but sinister example of bureaucratic beastliness than to go to the other end of the scale and bludgeon the reader with one of numberless ghastly stories of German reprisals against civilians in occupied countries – some hideous incident like the burning to death of 600 women and children by a handful of SS men in a fit of pique.

Was it all worth it? There is no answer to such a question. Some people believed that any sacrifice was worthwhile if it disrupted the German war effort, however slightly. Others would take a more relative view, but would find themselves floundering in some impossible conundrum: how many innocent hostages to be shot for the death of a German soldier; how many streets burned and blasted to cripple one tank?

The most useful task which militant resistance could perform, from the point of view of Allied Forces Command, was to damage or destroy certain strategic targets, in particular communications. More damage could sometimes be done by the saboteur than by a squadron of bombers with fifty times as much explosive. Regular military leaders, especially Air Force leaders, perhaps tended to overrate the effect of the bomber, the subject of exaggerated fears in the 1930s, but sabotage also could be overrated. On the whole, the most remarkable aspect in stories of bridges demolished, dams broken, factories bombed, etc., whether by air or on the ground, is the speed with which the damage was rectified.

There were certain targets, regarded by the Allies as militarily important, which could only be attacked from the ground: two well-known examples are the Norwegian heavy-water plant and the French wolfram mines (though the former was also attacked by bombers). There were examples of the resistance calling in Allied aircraft to perform tasks which, on the face of it, would appear to belong to the sphere of the saboteur – precision attacks on individual buildings such as a Gestapo HQ in the middle of a city. In general, bombing was far more destructive of civilian lives and property than sabotage, but sabotage, unless it could be disguised in some way, could lead to savage reprisals by the occupation forces.

The total effect of sabotage by militant resistance groups during the Second World War would be impossible to calculate accurately. It was not very great, perhaps even insignificant. Even the two examples mentioned in the preceding paragraph, which Professor Alan S. Milward, an authority on the wartime economics of occupied countries, cites as rare examples of strategically or economically effective resistance activity, were really less important than they seemed at the time. The Germans would not have developed a nuclear bomb by 1945 even if the heavy-water supplies had not been disrupted, and the quantity of tungsten that Germany lost by attacks on the French wolfram mines was not enough to make a significant difference to war production.

If resistance operations against industrial or military targets were of minor importance from the overall strategic viewpoint, so were activities against enemy troops. Certainly there were cases of the Germans being compelled to move a division or two of first-class troops into occupied countries in order to contain partisans, but the total numbers were not large, and it would be hard to demonstrate a single example of a serious weakening of the German front line through this cause. Nowhere, of course, did partisans tackle the Germans on equal terms. That is not the purpose of the guerrilla, whose function is to harass, or raid, and then swiftly withdraw. When irregular troops did become involved in a face-to-face fight with the Germans, it was usually (not always) as a result of a deliberate German attack on their territory, and unless they received rapid and powerful help from outside, it almost invariably ended in disaster for the irregulars.

It is doubtful, however, if the main importance of militant resistance operations against the enemy can be measured in terms of strategic or economic damage, or in any material terms. The effect of such operations on the enemy is perhaps less vital than their effect on those who carry them out. Once the numbness induced by the initial shock of conquest was past, many people found it impossible to carry on under the new regime as though nothing had happened. Even those who did so–the vast majority naturally–often felt a deep, concealed resentment and, if never actually engaged in resistance themselves, identified with those who were. Others no less naturally resented the trouble brought upon themselves by the activities of their resisting compatriots, either in the form of reprisals by the enemy, or more directly the exploitation, threats, and blackmail of the resisters themselves.

The reputation of resistance is mixed. In the Soviet Union, nothing is more honourable than service as a partisan in the Great Patriotic War. Similarly in Yugoslavia, unless of course you were a Četnik rather than a Titoist; or in Albania, unless you were a Zogist, and so on. In France you are not necessarily regarded as a hero if you were a *maquisard*. In certain circles in Greece to remark that a man was in the resistance is as tactless as saying he was in prison.

'It would be absurd,' says M.R.D. Foot, a British historian of wartime resistance, 'to maintain that everybody was in resistance for good conscientious reasons. There were plenty of rascals ... some plain bandits ... some scroungers' ('What Good did Resistance Do?', Stephen Hawes and Ralph White (eds.) *Resistance in Europe 1939-45*, 1975). So there are in any large group of people no doubt. Militant resistance, with its rejection of established authority and therefore of law, brought out the best and the worst in people. Though resistance is not to blame–for it did not often descend to the depth of vileness of the system it opposed–it is not fanciful to suggest a connection between it and the activities of terrorist groups which perpetrate so many acts of savagery in the world today.

Above: After the Italians invaded Greece from Albania in November 1940 the Greeks drove them back and occupied part of southern Albania. Here a Greek soldier talks to Albanian peasants in the liberated region.

Below: Much of the Albanian army withdrew with its weapons to Yugoslavia in the face of the Italian invasion of April 1939; there was no hope of successful resistance to the well-equipped conquerors.

Albania

THE NOTORIOUS REMARK of the British prime minister, Neville Chamberlain, about Czechoslovakia—'a far-away country of which we know nothing'—might have been better applied to Albania, which was even farther away and much more of a mystery. But Chamberlain was of course being disingenuous. Even Albania was not entirely a closed book to certain departments of the British government; there were plenty of British agents scattered throughout the Balkans in the 1930s. Nevertheless, Albania, with a total population hardly exceeding one million, was rather obscure. It was remarkably backward even by Balkan standards, never mind the standards of Western Europe, and except for a very small intellectual minority and in one or two towns, the general state of society might have been compared to the more remote parts of tropical Africa, or to Western Europe in the 15th century. Only about one third of children in Albania between the world wars received education *of any kind.* There were no railways in the whole country except for a couple of short lengths like that linking Tirana and Durazzo, and in the relatively prosperous Mati valley British officers in 1944 found the windows of most of the houses unglazed.

Albania is a small country but it occupies an important strategic position opposite the 'heel' of Italy, commanding the entrance to the Adriatic Sea. It has comparatively few obvious advantages otherwise (though the Germans were interested in its chrome supplies), but this alone was enough to make it vulnerable to the manoeuvres of the great powers engaged in expanding or maintaining their power and to ensure that it would remain under some kind of foreign domination. For centuries Albania was part of the domain of the Ottoman Turks; hence the preponderance of Muslims in the population. Not until the Balkan War in the early 20th century did the country gain a brief moment of independence, under an obscure German prince who was installed as king. He lasted only six months, and soon afterwards Albania was engulfed in the Great War. However, although Albania had never, except for that brief moment (and for a short time under the great national hero Scanderbeg in the 16th century) enjoyed independence as a state, neither the Turks nor any other foreign power had ever succeeded in subjugating the country totally. The mountain people, far removed from the centres of military and political power, remained independent in all essentials, and guerrilla warfare was a way of life for them long before the Second World War began.

In 1914, southern Albania was occupied by Greece, while the Italians took the strategic port of Valona, and the north was overrun by the Serbs. The latter were soon driven out by Austro-Hungarian troops, and Austria was regarded by Albanian nationalists as the power most sympathetic to them. However, the collapse of the Austro-Hungarian Empire meant that, at the end of the war, Albania seemed likely to become part of the victors' spoils, to be apportioned to those of its more powerful neighbours who could assert the strongest claim. Circumstances, not least the determination of the Albanian themselves, prevented this, and Albania's independence was restored, though the Italians had to be ejected by force.

As in so many other new states, parliamentary democracy did not flourish in Albania. The problems were mostly the familiar ones of second-rate and selfish men struggling for the corrupt fruits of power, but there were additional internal divisions in Albania which, together with the general backwardness of the country, caused special problems. In particular, the Albanians were (and are, no doubt) not one people but two, the Ghegs and the Tosks, who speak different dialects and inhabit respectively the north and the south of the country. The Ghegs lived in beautiful but very poor country, scratching a living on the mountainsides. They were chiefly Muslims, although there was an important Roman Catholic group in the north-west. Their society has been compared with that of the Scottish clans in the early 18th century, with the chiefs commanding autocratic powers over their followers. The Tosks were mainly poor peasants but included the – very few–industrial workers. Their chief men were the big landowners, and they too were mainly Muslim. There was a Greek Orthodox minority in the south, which was linked with Albanians living beyond the border in Greece itself. There was an even larger Albanian minority living in the Kossovo district, at that time part of Yugoslavia. This was to cause some future difficulties for Albanian partisans.

Although there were no political parties in the usual sense of the term, there were two rival groups which it would be easy though misleading to regard as representing the Right and the Left. The big landowners and chiefs mostly adhered to Ahmet Zogu, himself a member of a powerful Gheg family and by far the most efficient and ruthless politician in the country. The other group, which contained liberal reformers and radicals, was led by the American-educated Orthodox bishop, Fan Noli. In 1925 Zogu gained power when, with the help of Yugoslavia and some White Russian troops, he overthrew the regime of Fan Noli (who had himself come to power by a coup against Zogu the previous year). He instituted an authoritarian

SCUTARI
TIRANA
DURAZZO
VALONA
KORITZA
YANNINA
SALONICA
CORFU
Pindus Mts
LARISSA
Gorgopotamos Bridge
Asopos Viaduct
PATRAS
PELOPONNESE
ATHENS
KALAMATA
NAUPLION
HERAKLION
CRETE

✕✕✕ Limit of Greek Advance
Areas over 500 metres
╫╫╫ Railways

regime and at first encouraged better relations with Italy. Albania soon became alarmingly dependent on the Italians, both economically (the little industry that existed was mostly in Italian hands), and militarily (the Albanian army was mainly officered by Italians). Zogu, who in 1927 enhanced the somewhat Ruritanian image of his country by the grandiose gesture of making himself king as Zog I, endeavoured to limit the encroaching influence of Italy by, for example, appointing British officers to train the police force. However, resentment against the growing Italian influence was one of the causes of several minor revolts (though probably domestic conflicts made a larger contribution) in the 1930s. Efforts to restrict Italian control of education and military training offended Mussolini, and Italian financial aid was cut off, but only for a short time. Albania needed Italy, and an agreement was patched up.

In 1939 Mussolini decided he must quickly do something towards creating his new Roman Empire and stop Hitler getting all the glory, and as a first step towards it he invaded Albania–an easy option and a necessary step towards the envisaged Balkan empire–on 7 April, Good Friday. Except at Durazzo, where there was brief but fierce resistance led by Abbas Kupi, the Italians encountered little difficulty, and within a few days the country was occupied. Zog fled to Greece, eventually to London, and a puppet government was installed in Tirana.

The mountains, however, remained remote and there was widespread resentment of the Italians not so much through injured nationalism (though nationalism had certainly grown during the generation of independence) as through the ancient unpopularity of the Italians in Albania. On Independence Day, in November, there were demonstrations against the Italians in the towns. The Italian attack on Greece, which ended with the Greeks occupying part of Albania, did nothing to placate the Albanians as the Greeks seemed to think that they were reclaiming territory rightfully theirs. In the north however, following the German break-up of Yugoslavia, Kossovo was given to Albania.

As in other countries, resistance to the occupation by enemy forces was slow to get started, as most people were too bewildered and too preoccupied with adjusting to the changed circumstances to think of any concerted action. One of the earliest active leaders was Abbas Kupi. After his gallant action at Durazzo he had fled abroad, but he returned, after an approach by the British, to his native Kruya, where he had been a popular administrator (in spite of the fact that he could neither read nor write) under King Zog. With one or two other prominent Albanian exiles and a handful of armed men Abbas Kupi crossed into Albania from Yugoslavia in April 1941. They recruited more men in Muslim territory, and though unsuccessful in the Catholic areas, they were able to attack the odd Italian patrol. Unfortunately, they had not planned for the German conquest of Yugoslavia, which was completed within a matter of days after they had entered Albania and left them completely isolated. The movement collapsed and the leaders hastily dispersed. Abbas Kupi make his way to his own town of Kruya in central Albania, where he was unlikely to be betrayed, and gradually built up support, or at least sympathy, in the surrounding villages. The Italians, after making one attempt to lure him to their side, were keen to catch him, and nearly succeeded on at least one occasion, when he shot his way out of an ambush. Though the winter was hard, and almost all Abbas Kupi's followers temporarily deserted him, in the spring he began to attract much larger numbers from a wide area.

The German invasion of Russia released Albanian Communists from earlier inhibitions and, as in neighbouring countries, they soon became prominent in organizing resistance. Fan Noli's party had kept up some link with the Comintern in the 1920s, and former followers of the Bishop were active in setting up Communist cells in the 1930s. But there was never a single party organization, and to a large extent the Albanian Communist Party was the creation of Operation Barbarossa plus the efforts of certain Yugoslav Communists, who were influential in Albania from the first. The general secretary of the party was an ex-schoolteacher in his thirties named Enver Hoxha, who came from Korcha, the chief Communist stronghold. Though falling far short of Tito's stature, Hoxha shared with him the qualities of toughness, cleverness and the capacity to survive.

The Communists were stronger in the south, where social conditions— among the Tosk peasantry, the industrial proletariat (what there was of it) and a small but influential number of foreign-educated younger people— were more congenial. The Gheg clan system was less receptive to Communism, while all attempts to organize resistance in the north were somewhat hampered by the fact that conditions were better under the Italians than under Zog, since the recovery of the Kossovo had made food cheaper and more abundant. On the other hand, the Italians were resented as foreigners, and the Albanians in general, traditionally not at all a law-abiding people, resented any attempt at regimentation.

By the spring of 1942 there were a number of centrally organized partisan units in the south whose leadership was undoubtedly Communist, though in the customary manner, great stress was laid upon the non-ideological character of the movement and on its non-Communist members. Besides these groups there were Abbas Kupi's followers in central Albania and a couple of smaller groups led by Gheg chieftains in the north. The Communists took the lead in forming a united front in which these groups were included, which was called the National Liberation Movement (LNC, later FNC). The most significant effect of the formation of this body was that it gave the Communists, who had a majority in the executive committee, power in the north, where the Gheg chiefs were out-manoeuvered by Moscow-trained agents. Only Abbas Kupi managed to hold on to his independence in his own territory.

The strength of Communism among the Tosks prompted the creation of the *Balli Kombëtar* (National Front), conservative, though republican (the Tosks never liked Zog), comparatively non-ideological, but opposed to Communism and therefore potentially hostile to the LNC. *Balli Kombëtar* began to carry out some acts of sabotage in late 1942. They were less active on the whole than the LNC, and perhaps more inclined to weigh the cost of their activities against likely reprisals. However, neither organization was really of any economic or strategic significance at this time.

There were other sources of conflict, besides ideological, between LNC and *Balli Kombëtar*. The Ballist leaders, strongly nationalist, were determined to hold on to Kossovo after the war. The Communists, under strong Yugoslav influence, seemed unlikely to do so. Kossovo also deterred the Ballists to some extent from full commitment to the Allied cause, as it was the Axis who had given Kossovo to Albania and an Allied victory, though otherwise desirable, might lead to its loss.

Top left: Abbas Kupi found his resistance movement weakened by British prevarication.

Top right: King Zog united the country in the 1920s and 1930s and began to modernize the administration and communications.

Above: A session of the small and fairly weak Albanian parliament at Tirana in 1938.

Top: A traditional gathering of Albanian chieftains and tribesmen; the abortive meeting of Balli Kombëtar and Communist leaders in 1943 took a similar form.

Above: The Italian forces in Albania in retreat from the invading Greeks in 1941.

There ensued a sharp crescendo of guerrilla war against the Italians, who were badly shaken and eventually responded with hysterical reprisals, in turn provoking more Albanian attacks. However, the Italians rallied and were regaining the initiative when the armistice was signed removing Italy from the Axis. Some Italian units marched north to Yugoslavia; others joined the LNC where, as in Yugoslavia, they were disarmed after an initially friendly reception; some units simply fell apart—it is said, for instance by Julian Amery (*Sons of the Eagle,* London 1948), that some Italian soldiers were sold as slave-labourers in the Albanian mountains. At any rate, one indisputable result of the Italian surrender was that the partisans came into possession of a considerable quantity of arms and equipment, and they were soon in possession of large parts of the country. Some places, such as the region around Valona, were taken over by the *Balli Kombëtar*, and in Kruya Abbas Kupi reigned supreme. The remaining Italian garrisons were on the point of negotiating their surrender to British military missions when the Germans acted.

With their usual efficiency, Hitler's troops snatched the apple dropped by the Italians before it could fall into the mouth of the Allies. Paratroopers landed in Tirana and quickly cleared the district. Abbas Kupi was thrown out of Kruya again after a sharp battle, while more German troops drove into LNC territory from Macedonia and sent the partisans scurrying again into the hills. Within a few days, the Albanians had lost all the towns they had taken and were again reduced to a somewhat ineffective force of mountain guerrillas.

The last thing the Germans wanted was another hostile country to occupy. Apart from the coast and perhaps the chrome supplies, they had no interest in Albania, and therefore hoped that the Albanians would govern themselves with a minimal German military presence. Apart from some fierce actions where guerrillas were known to have been busy, the Germans accordingly acted with moderation. Smiling sweetly, they assured the Albanians that they were the true successors of the Austrian Empire, which Albanians had regarded as a friendly patron. They set up a new government under Medhi Frasheri, a widely respected politician; legislation passed under Italian auspices was abolished, an amnesty declared for those who had fought the Italians, and, most remarkably, the new government declared that Albania was neutral (difficult to maintain in view of the presence of German troops, even if there was not a great number, but a parallel could be drawn with Egypt where British troops were no less numerous). The new policy had a certain amount of success. The Germans were not generally loathed in Albania, as the Italians were, and the new neutral government managed to attract a good deal of support, from members of the *Balli Kombëtar,* among others. Thus, when in October 1943 the LNC partisans began to attack rival guerrilla groups, Enver Hoxha was able to say with some truth that he was only acting against collaborators.

The Allies, more particularly the British, were not convinced by this protest, yet their policy tended to favour the LNC. As LNC was the largest and most active group, it had throughout received the lion's share of British supplies (it is still something of a mystery why Abbas Kupi, who was on the whole remarkably loyal to the British, received such niggardly treatment). The *faux-naif* British policy of maintaining a state of neutrality, if not ignorance, concerning the internal affairs of the occupied country they were concerned with, and corresponding emphasis on 'the chaps who are killing the most Jerries' was particularly inappropriate in Albania. Britain had virtually approved Mussolini's takeover of Albania in 1939 by saying nothing and by refusing to recognize the exiled King Zog as rightful ruler (despite his presence in London). Currently, while doing everything possible to encourage Albanian partisans, the British had no long-term policy on Albania, no evident interest in what would happen after the war. (It might be pointed out, however, that Stalin did not show much interest in Albania either; Albania did not figure in the crude bargaining for postwar influence between Stalin and Churchill in which Yugoslavia and Greece both figured prominently.)

The LNC partisans were swiftly able to clear the countryside of Ballist guerrillas, who took refuge in the German-occupied towns. The Germans, eager to encourage civil war, gave some of them weapons to go back to the mountains and fight the LNC. Meanwhile, the LNC attack had shown the Gheg leaders what they could expect, and Abbas Kupi withdrew from LNC in December 1943 to form his own movement, sometimes called the Legality movement or, for its members' monarchist loyalties, the Zogists. A clash with the LNC was prevented for the time being by a German offensive against the partisans followed by the onset of a particularly cold winter, during which Abbas Kupi's guerrillas temporarily retired to their villages.

Early in 1944 guerrilla activities seemed to be almost at a standstill. Virtually nothing was happening in the north; in central Albania Abbas Kupi was quiescent; in the south the partisans' numbers had shrunk considerably, and their control was limited to remote areas. During the course of the year, however, this situation was to be transformed, as the LNC steadily expanded from its strongholds in the south to control an ever-widening area.

In the spring of 1944 it was already clear to Abbas Kupi and other Zogist leaders that the Germans were soon going to lose the war, and that the Germans and their Albanian collaborators were much less of a threat to them than the Communists. This naturally did not predispose them towards renewing the attack on the occupation forces. At the same time they were—and had reason to be—disillusioned with the British. The rising of the previous year had been undertaken in hope of an Allied landing in Albania. No landing had occurred, and the rising had fizzled out. The

British, moreover, were not making the right noises over Albania's southern border. Like the Americans they upheld the principle of national sovereignty and free elections, but they also said that frontiers should be decided after the war and to the Albanians this sounded as though Britain was preparing to force them into making concessions to Greece (the first British liaison officers who entered Albania from the south were for a time taken to be Greek spies). Thus, neither of the main Albanian resistance groups, in spite of friendly relations at a personal level, was especially warm towards the British. Whenever the British gave any support to *Balli Kombëtar,* Enver Hoxha accused them of favouring the forces of reaction, in spite of the fact that the British gave much greater support to his own movement (thus making it easier for him after 1945 to turn the country into the repellent totalitarian state it is now.) Moreover, it was clear to the British from an early stage that the Communist leaders of the LNC were more interested in eliminating their rivals among fellow-Albanians than in fighting the Italians (and, indeed, that Gheg guerrillas were more concerned to check Communism than fight the Germans).

During the spring and summer of 1943, as the Italians were seen to be faltering, more Albanians joined the resistance organizations. The Communists, calculating that there might shortly be an Allied invasion of the Balkans which would jeopardise their future plans, increased their activities against the Ballists. Abbas Kupi, who had some influence with both organizations though his aims were opposed to both, attempted to act as mediator, bringing the sides together, as the British were also trying to do. A meeting of leaders of both sides took place in the mountains east of Tirana in July 1943. It is unlikely that anything would have come of this meeting had it not been for the news, which arrived while discussions were in progress in an apple orchard, of the fall of Mussolini. In the ensuing euphoria, the two sides enthusiastically agreed to co-operate without restriction in attacks on the Italian forces. Needless to say, this amiable spirit soon evaporated, but at least it suggested that co-operation between the rival Albanian irregulars was not impossible.

Now the British were saying that they would drop no arms to the Zogists, who were desperately short of them, unless they showed by their actions that they were prepared to renew their attacks on the Germans. Abbas Kupi might have recognised Catch 22: he needed British arms to fight the Germans, but the British would not give him arms *until* he fought the Germans. Moreover, the British were still making no commitments about the future of Albania, and they were still ostentatiously supporting the LNC. True, the LNC were fighting the Germans, and the Zogists were not. But as the Zogists complained, watching a British aeroplane dropping supplies to LNC units on their way to attack them, nine out of ten rounds supplied to Enver Hoxha's battalions were fired at Albanians, not Germans. The Germans, too, were not hated as the Italians were hated, and the difficult business of raising guerrilla forces among the tribes, making promises here, bargaining there, here dropping a few threats, there flattering a few egos–became so much harder. There was really no motive for Abbas Kupi and his fellow Gheg chiefs to attack the Germans, bar one: they needed British support. In spite of some earlier disillusionment, many of them still believed that Britain would prevent a Communist takeover of their country. Britain was a great sea power, one Albanian leader told Julian Amery, and Albania had an important sea coast which could not be ceded to a hostile power. Others, perhaps including Abbas Kupi himself, were less sanguine. Yet they had no choice. It was the British or nothing.

Perhaps, as Anton Logoreci remarks (*The Albanians,* London 1977), the political future of Albania was really settled when Britain chose to give its full backing to Tito's Partisan movement. The Albanians, to some extent disciples and pupils of the Yugoslav Partisans, benefitted equally. The British were unwilling to do anything that would harm their relations with the LNC, which they correctly saw as the most powerful anti-Fascist force in the country, and though they tried quite seriously to create a united front among all Albanian resistance groups, Hoxha could afford to take a hard line. He refused to have anything to do with 'fascists' and 'collaborators' like the Zogists.

The LNC advanced, and Abbas Kupi was forced to retreat. Each time he retreated his strength was correspondingly diminished, because he could only command support by personal leadership, and when he departed from a district and the LNC moved in, support swiftly dropped away. He did renew attacks on the Germans, and the British did promise to drop arms and supplies, but the total amounted to one load of explosives for a particular operation, while the Zogists found themselves forced to fight on two fronts. One Zogist group was in the process of ambushing a German convoy, had knocked out the two leading vehicles and was shooting it out with an armoured car, when they were attacked in the back by an LNC partisan unit. They naturally broke off their attack on the convoy and refused to resume actions against the Germans henceforth. Such actions, apart from loot, offered the guerrillas nothing whatsoever, since by this time the Germans were retreating from Albania as fast as possible.

The final stroke of horrid irony for Abbas Kupi came when the partisans had taken over his whole area and he, with one or two friends and attendants, was reduced to a few square miles on the coast, with enemies all around. The British headquarters in Bali told their horrified men on the spot–the liaison officers who had been with Abbas Kupi for the previous six months and had formed the highest respect for his honour and gallantry–that they would not evacuate him. Such a move, they explained, would be resented by Enver Hoxha. This order was subsequently reversed, though by that time Abbas Kupi had made his own escape–by an unreliable boat which reached Brindisi after six days adrift in the Adriatic. 'The future is dark', he told his British friends, 'but one day you will be strong again. I still put my trust in England.'

*Czechs fighting in the streets during the
Prague Rising of May 1945. Virtually
unarmed and not supported by the
Allies, thousands of Czechs died in the
Rising.*

Czechoslovakia

THE STATE OF CZECHOSLOVAKIA emerged from the ruins of the Habsburg empire after the Great War. It was the most successful of the new states created after 1918, and under President Masaryk and his successor, Edvard Beneš, it was politically one of the most stable states in Europe in the 1920s and 1930s, besides being economically prosperous. It was not, however, a homogeneous nation. It consisted of four historical regions, from west to east, Bohemia, Moravia, Slovakia and Ruthenia, and contained large minorities of other nations, such as the Germans who inhabited parts of Bohemia adjacent to Germany. It was these people whom Hitler asserted to be in need of his protection. The notorious Munich agreement of September 1938 hived off the area known as the Sudetenland and incorporated it within Hitler's Reich.

The main internal problem for Czechoslovakia during its 20 years of independence sprang not from the relatively small sections of disgruntled Germans, or Hungarians or other minorities, but from the conflict between the Czechs and Slovaks. Many Slovaks were never reconciled to fusion with the Czechs and, rightly or wrongly, tended to regard themselves as subjects of Czech exploitation.

During the weeks of rising tension that preceded the Munich agreement, the Czechs, while remaining open to reason and discussion, showed signs that they were not prepared to cave in before Hitler's shrieks of self-righteous protest. However, once the German-Czech problem became an international affair, and Neville Chamberlain decided he must save the peace of Europe at almost any cost, Czechoslovakia was doomed. It has often been said that if the Czechs had (literally) stuck to their guns, Hitler might have found himself in serious trouble, for it would have been difficult for France to avoid fulfilling her treaty obligations to come to the aid of the Czechs, while Britain perforce would have followed France; more to the point, Czechoslovakia, far from being defenceless, was probably better prepared for war in 1938 than any other country in Europe, including Germany. The Czech army of 35 divisions was, in 1938, scarcely smaller than the German army and the Czechs had better armour and artillery. The Czech armaments industry was one of the best in Europe (the bren gun was a Czech invention), and the Czech frontier defences were regarded by no less a body than the German general staff as formidable. The Munich agreement ensured that these assets, which included approximately 1,500 aircraft, 800 tanks and 2,250 pieces of field artillery, would pass to Germany, not to Germany's opponents, in the approaching war.

The archetypal Czech hero is the Good Soldier Schweik—amiable and apparently obtuse, crafty in the avoidance of trouble. It is thus that the Czechs have survived as a small nation among bigger and more aggressive peoples, not by throwing their weight about. There was therefore little chance that Beneš would resist the arrangement thrust upon him at Munich, though he more than anyone realised what it meant.

The Good Soldier Schweik, willing but crafty, infuriates an army officer.

After Munich Beneš resigned, and Czechoslovakia rapidly fell apart. Poland and Hungary, jackals following the German lion, lopped off small sections to which they had more or less doubtful claims. Slovakia and Ruthenia claimed virtual independence. Czech forces were demobilised under German pressure and on 15 March 1939 the Germans rang down the curtain on the grim farce when they marched into Prague.

When war broke out slightly less than a year after Munich, the Czechs seemed to be thoroughly cowed. The Germans despised them, and anyway thought, not unnaturally, that as the Czechs had not fought to defend their country before it was invaded, they would not start fighting now that it was conquered and crushed. They were wrong, however. The Czechs no longer felt alone and isolated; Germany now had other opponents, and there were nationalist demonstrations on Independence Day (28 October) in several places, ruthlessly suppressed. Demonstrations at Charles University provoked the shut-down of all Czech universities throughout the war. Nine students were shot without trial. They were selected arbitrarily by the Gestapo; one of them was secretary of the Union for Co-operation with the Germans.

In London, Beneš set up a Czech government in exile, though it was not without difficulty that he got himself recognized as the chief representative of a free Czechoslovakia which, he insisted, remained in existence despite the German takeover in Prague. For there was a semi-puppet government in Prague which was recognized, not only by Britain, France and other sovereign states, but even, in a sense, by Beneš. He let it be known that he would expect the Prague government to resign whenever they could do more to help the Czechs out of office than in it, while the Prague government refrained from criticising Beneš and his colleagues in London. The Germans were quite well aware of the contact between the Prague government and London, but for the time being they preferred to ignore it. Despite such excesses as those against the students mentioned above, they were still anxious to gain Czech co-operation, and therefore avoided too much provocation. The German 'Protector', Konstantin von Neurath, was relatively benign, though the 'State Secretary', Karl Hermann Frank, favoured a tougher, more repressive policy.

As in other occupied countries, the underground in Bohemia and Moravia began as entirely unorganized discussion between angry groups and individuals, with no central command, no precise policy, and worst of all, very little security. Various political groups were involved, and not all of them supported whole-heartedly the exile government of Beneš. Nevertheless, there was remarkably full communication between London and the Czech underground in the early days, conducted at first largely by businessmen travelling to neutral countries and, from September 1940, increasingly by radio. The Czechs, who had fallen into rather hopeless gloom after Munich, had recovered themselves by the time the war started, and underground activity was more widespread and more vigorous than in most other occupied countries during the early stages of the war. There was a general feeling that Naziism would be a short-lived phenomenon and that a German defeat was imminent. This belief in a quick German defeat naturally contributed to the lack of security-consciousness in the undergound, which led to many arrests.

Meanwhile, the government, if not exactly collaborationist, encouraged acceptance of the New Order, again partly as a result of the belief that it would be brief. There were 27,000 entries in a competition for school-children organized by the Germans, though there was apparently no pressure to take part, and there was a marked increase in the demand for textbooks of German. Fear may have played a part in these and other signs of willingness to co-operate with the occupying power, but it is clear that in the population at large there was a good deal of what Vojtěch Mastný calls Schweikism (*The Czechs Under Nazi Rule*, 1971). And with the tide of German victories in full flood, resistance seemed pointless to many.

One very encouraging development, as far as resisters were concerned, was the growing coolness in German-Soviet relations, caused partly by the very success of German arms, which Stalin had not anticipated when he made his alliance with Hitler in August 1939. The Czechs were not anti-Russian and, on the whole, they were not particularly anti-Communist (Communists had taken part in parliamentary democracy in Czechoslovakia before the war.). In London, Beneš bent his considerable diplomatic skills to cementing close relations between Czechs and Russians and Jan Masaryk had never seen him so pleased about anything as he was when he learned of the German attack of Russia, which meant that the Soviet Union entered the war on the Allied side.

Within a few months of Operation Barbarossa, the Russians had dropped agents into Bohemia, but all of them appear to have been quickly captured. The British also dropped agents at about the same time: at the end of 1941 SOE was stepping up operations in all occupied countries. But the effectiveness of Czech resistance was exaggerated outside the country. Organization was still comparatively patchy, and many individuals fell into the hands of the Gestapo. There were virtually no weapons, so that British inquiries about the possibility of an armed rising in Bohemia and Moravia to coincide with a German retreat were hopelessly inappropriate. However, a good deal of sabotage was carried out against the Germans by the UVOD (*Ústřední vedení odboje domácího*), Central Command of Home Resistance. Fuel dumps were fired, trains derailed or otherwise damaged, and telephone lines cut. Explosives were manufactured secretly by the Communists, and strikes broke out with increasing frequency, though these were mainly the result of local economic grievances rather than central political planning. A boycott of the press in September 1941 was moderately successful, while the undergound press flourished. All in all, it was clear that the Czechs, far from quietly adapting themselves to fit into the pattern of Hitler's Greater Reich, were becoming increasingly troublesome to the occupying forces. Berlin decided to take the decision that Frank had long been urging – to end the namby-pamby treatment amiably supervized by von Neurath, and to get tough. Undoubtedly, Frank considered himself the ideal person to administer the latter policy, but Hitler, taking up a suggestion by Martin Bormann, found an even more suitable candidate, Reinhard Heydrich.

It is hard to imagine a more thoroughly loathsome group of men than the top men in Nazi Germany, and Heydrich was no less repellent than his patron, Himmler. Tall, vigorous and blond, he appeared the perfect 'Aryan' specimen, although it appears that one of his grandmothers was Jewish. He managed to suppress this–for a Nazi–shameful fact and, as the man chiefly responsible for evolving the 'Final Solution' to the Jewish 'problem', he showed no lack of zeal in his anti-Semitism. As head of the security service, including the Gestapo, Heydrich was a very powerful figure, and it would have seemed that to go to Prague as 'Protector' of Bohemia and Moravia was a considerable demotion, had it not been intended as a temporary post and had he not kept his other offices during his time in Prague.

Heydrich's policy was 'break and bend'. In other words, first terrify the people by violence and brutality and then, when they are cowed, it will be much easier to order their behaviour. Almost his first act was to arrest the prime minister, who was tried for treason and sentenced to death, though the sentence was not carried out for some months. The mayor of Prague suffered the same fate. These salutary examples were followed by arbitrary arrests, charges and trials before summary courts which could only condemn to death or – the same thing in the end – hand over to the Gestapo (they could also release, but that seldom happened). Heydrich also moved rapidly and effectively to eliminate Jews from the country. Nearly 100,000 Jews were deported from Bohemia and Moravia between 1941 and 1944; at the end of the war less than 4,000 of them were still alive. The Prague government became exclusively the creature of Berlin.

Acts of sabotage declined sharply during the winter of 1941-42, and the Germans were possibly correct in ascribing most of those that did take place to the Communists. The Communists seem to have been more successful than other members of the resistance at avoiding the worst of Heydrich's represson. But on the whole, Heydrich could claim fair success in 'pacifying' the Czech protectorate.

The assassination of Heydrich in May 1942, shortly before his intended return to Germany, was not provoked primarily by his repressive and brutal policy, nor by his comparative success against the Czech resistance. Planned in London by the Czech exiles, though with the advice and assistance of British intelligence agencies and SOE, it was first proposed soon after Heydrich's appointment to Prague. It was a propaganda exercise, to catch the attention of the world and boost Czech resistance.

The leaders of the team chosen to carry out this act were Jozef Gabčík, a Slovak, and Jan Kubiš. They were parachuted in during Christmas week 1941, and were followed by other agents trained, like themselves, by SOE. They made contact with the underground but did not tell anyone of their precise mission. When this did become known nearly five months later, the leaders of the native Czech resistance were horrified, and they signalled London urgently to request that the mission be cancelled. Their message made the following points. An attack on Heydrich personally, whether successful or not, could be of no benefit to the Allied cause; but it would be a disaster for the Czech people. All hostages and others in German hands would be immediately at risk. Thousands of others would be in equal danger, while the nation as a whole would be subjected to repression far more fierce than anything suffered hitherto. The resistance organization, already much depleted, would be destroyed utterly and future actions that might really be of use to the Allies would no longer be possible. This wholly accurate forecast notwithstanding, on 27 May the plan went into effect.

Heydrich, who was due in Berlin that night, was late leaving home for

Top left: After the war, Jozef Tiso, the collaborationist head of Slovakia, was sentenced to death.

Top right: Reinhard Heydrich took up office in Czechoslovakia on 27 September 1941 and was attacked exactly eight months later.

Above: A group of Czech partisans at their mountain hideout.

Opposite above: Josef Gabčík (left) and Jan Kubiš (right), the team that killed Heydrich, photographed after their deaths in the crypt of a Prague church.

Below: German soldiers completing the destruction of the village of Lidice in retaliation for the death of Heydrich.

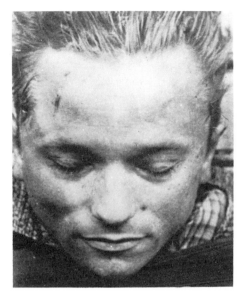

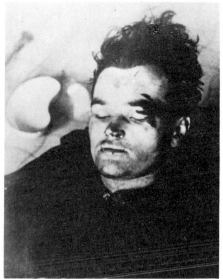

the office, and told his guards to go ahead. He followed a little later in an open car with only a chauffeur besides himself. On a sharp corner, where the car slowed down, Gabčík stepped into the road and levelled a submachine gun at him. As guns often do, it jammed at the worst possible moment, but Kubiš tossed a bomb into the car before evasive action could be taken. Heydrich was hurt, though not badly enough to prevent him chasing the would-be assassins with his automatic. They got away, Heydrich died unexpectedly a week later, of blood poisoning.

Within three hours of the attack of Heydrich's car, Hitler had telephoned Frank in Prague to demand the arrest and execution of 10,000 civilians (on Frank's advice he later rescinded this order). Martial law was proclaimed, huge rewards offered for information leading to an arrest, and grim hints dropped about what would happen if the culprits were not arrested. The summary courts went back into commission, and executions of entire families were carried out on such charges as 'approving' of attempted assassination. After Heydrich's death, and with Hitler's approval, the village of Lidice, whose name has become a symbol of the worst kind of atrocity, was completely destroyed. Male inhabitants were shot without exception. (One of them happened to be in hospital with a broken leg; the Germans waited until he came out and then shot him.) The women were sent to Ravensbruck concentration camp and the children, except for a dozen who were regarded as 'racially suitable' to be brought up as Germans in German foster homes, were also deported and later died in the gas chambers. The village was burned to the ground. Later, similar treatment was accorded to the smaller village of Ležáky.

Gabčík and Kubiš were eventually betrayed. They were surrounded by a large German force in the crypt of the Orthodox church of St Cyril in Prague, where they shot it out with their attackers for several hours.

The Germans committed worse crimes than that of Lidice, if degree in such horrors can be measured. Many more people were killed in revenge for Heydrich in the prisons than in that village. But the massacre at Lidice was publicised throughout the world, and showed beyond doubt what crimes the German leadership was coldly capable of committing. For the Nazis, the road from Lidice led to Nuremberg. The Czech government in exile had certainly succeeded in catching the world's attention (Lidice prompted a British disavowal of Munich), but at a cost that seems excessive. In the repression that followed Gabčík and Kubiš's bomb, what remained of the Czech underground was virtually wiped out. Practically the whole leadership of the Czech Communist Party also disappeared, while the network set up by Gabčík and Kubiš and other SOE agents in the months before the assassination collapsed. Although SOE later sent in more agents, they were engaged in intelligence work only. Total casualties, as a result of German reprisals for Heydrich's death, numbered about 2,000. In death, as Vojtěch Mastný wrote, Heydrich finally achieved his aim—the pacification of the Czech protectorate.

The situation in Slovakia was different. In March 1939, the Hitler-backed People's Party led by Mgr Jozef Tiso had secured complete independence from Czechoslovakia and voluntarily placed the country under German protection. Most Slovaks had not wanted to break up Czechoslovakia even if they *had* wanted a greater degree of autonomy, and a still smaller number wanted to be 'protected' by Hitler.

The Tiso government, like some other collaborationist regimes, grew out of its infatuation with the Germans fairly quickly. Anti-German activities by members of the banned Agrarian party, largely Protestant and middle-class, and even by the Communists were ignored by the Slovak minister of home affairs, formerly fanatically pro-Nazi. The army commander even considered a plan to take his forces over to the Russians.

Unlike Bohemia which is comparatively flat except for border regions, Slovakia is a suitable country for guerrilla warfare, and when the Germans were forced to retreat in 1944, partisan activity increased.

In August 1944 the Germans began the military occupation of Slovakia. They announced that they were coming at the request of Tiso's government to restore order, in face of increasing activity by partisans, often led by Soviet officers who had been parachuted into the country in preceding months. The general uprising planned by the resistance leaders then took place, but to some extent the Germans had pre-empted it, and they succeeded in disarming two divisions of the Slovak army before they could act. The partisans, under General Jan Golian, were pushed back into the mountainous centre of the country. This region was proclaimed 'Free Slovakia', with its capital at Banská Bystrica. The government calling itself the Slovak National Council, announced its adherence to the Allied cause, its aim of restoring a pre-Munich Czechoslovakia, and its detestation of the Tiso regime. General Rudolf Viest was flown in from London to take command of the armed forces, Golian becoming his deputy.

With the Germans advancing in strength upon Free Slovakia from almost every direction, the revolt was in desperate need of Allied assistance. Since the decisions taken at the Teheran conference, Czechoslovakia had been assigned to the Soviet sphere of interest and the Slovak insurgents therefore depended, like the Poles, primarily on Russian help. And like the Poles, they were disappointed. Although the Russian armies were hardly more than 100 miles away, they showed no inclination to hasten their advance. On the contrary, they did not overrun Slovakia until the following spring. There was a military explanation, or at least excuse, for the delay, in the shape of stiff German resistance (one Russian advance was defeated at Ducla), and it is true that the Russians did provide rather more aid than they gave to Warsaw; but it was still too little and too late. Representatives of the Slovak National Council were kept hanging about in Moscow and finally returned with only vague promises of help. Russian equipment sent in amounted to 150 anti-tank rifles, 350 infantry rifles, explosives and a few aircraft—but no fuel to fly them. After a considerable delay, they also flew in the Czechoslovak airborne brigade of 2,800 men, formed in exile in the Soviet Union under Colonel Vladimír Prǐkryl, but they did not keep it supplied although they found aircraft to transport various Communist politicians and commissars into Free Slovakia. The Russians showed a bias against the professional Slovak forces and in favour of partisan bands, many of which were commanded by Soviet officers. There was a little aid from the British and the Americans, which might have been greater if the Russians had not refused to make airfields available to their supposed allies.

In the middle of October a change of government in Budapest allowed the Germans to attack through Hungary, and the situation of Free Slovakia, already fighting a desperate defence, became precarious. In two weeks, the remaining towns including Banská Bystrica had to be evacuated, and national resistance declined into the actions of small partisan bands in the mountains. These partisans included, besides Czechs and Slovaks, Yugoslavs, Bulgarians, Frenchmen (escaped prisoners of war, who fought with great panache), and of course Russians.

The Germans, supported by the collaborationist authorities, treated the Slovaks, whether partisans or not, with barbarous ferocity. They burned villages, destroyed property, transported thousands to concentration camps, and murdered many prisoners, including Generals Viest and Golian, who were captured at the beginning of November. Among others killed were all fifteen members of a US military mission, a British officer and two Associated Press correspondents – all of them in uniform. One mass grave discovered after the war contained 4,316 corpses.

In spite of Beneš's good relations with the Soviet Union, he was not able to persuade the Russians to bring much help to the insurgents in Slovakia, nor was he able to prevent the absorption of Trans-Carpathian Ruthenia, the easternmost province of Czechoslovakia, into the USSR, after considerable 'popular' agitation to that end. There was an obvious danger that Slovakia would suffer the same fate, and in March Beneš left London for Moscow, giving the Russians the opportunity of restoring what they acknowledged as Czechoslovakia's rightful government. Meanwhile the Red Army was on the move again. During April, it advanced through Moravia into Bohemia, and on 5 May Prague rose in revolt in anticipation of the Russian conquest.

The rising began with a rash of acts of defiance against the Germans – tearing down of German notices and pasting up of portraits of Tomáš Masaryk, the burning of German books, etc. The Czech police seized the radio station, taking the German guards by surprise, and broadcast appeals for help. Hundreds poured into the city from the surrounding country, and nearly 2,000 barricades were erected in the streets.

The fighting, much of it between virtually unarmed civilians on one side and tanks on the other, lasted for only about three days. Everyone knew the war was ending, and Prague was in chaos. The National Council, the body formally in charge of the rising, had only been formed a week or two earlier. It contained strong Communist representation and though it also included a representative of Beneš, it tended to keep its distance from the Czech government in exile. Many responsible leaders in Prague would have preferred to wait for liberation at the hands of the advancing armies.

Although tanks were used, as in Warsaw, the Germans did not embark on a major destruction of the city according to Hitler's orders. Nevertheless, they acted with savagery towards the civilian population of Prague, and German atrocities in the last stages of the war in Bohemia provoked corresponding acts against Germans living within Czechoslovakia, of whom all the survivors were eventually expelled from post-war Czechoslovakia. Czech casualties during the Rising approached 8,000, and they would have been worse but for the assistance of the Russian partisan army commanded by General A.A. Vlasov.

Vlasov commanded two divisions of anti-Soviet renegades who had supported the Germans but, during the Russian advance in the spring, had refused to fight with the Germans against the Red Army, and had torn off the German army insignia that they wore on their uniforms. At the time of the Rising, they were only about thirty miles from Prague and torn by conflicting loyalties and ambitions. In the event they decided to fight with the Czechs against their former masters, and despite their fast-disintegrating discipline, rendered valuable service. Afterwards, they became something of an embarrassment. Most of them filtered westward in small groups, in order to avoid having to surrender to the Red Army. Vlasov himself was captured by the Russians and subsequently executed.

The Red Army finally entered Prague on 9 May, two days after the official end of the war, although some fighting was still going on and it was the turn of Germans to fight as guerrillas and partisan bands. By that time, the rising had been, in effect, a failure, as the Germans had not been compelled to surrender by the insurgents, and the latter had suffered incomparably greater casualties. Amid the welter of slaughter of the previous five years, here was yet another vast and unnecessary sacrifice. When the Rising began, the Americans were not much more than fifty miles from Prague, and their advance had acquired an unstoppable momentum. However, by agreement with the Russians, the Americans were to proceed no farther than Pilsen. Eisenhower suggested to the Russians that he might let his men continue to Prague, which would certainly have saved many lives, but the Russians would not hear of it. Nor were the Americans particularly keen on the plan.

At any rate, it was the Russians who liberated Czechoslovakia, and Beneš had a far from easy task in establishing his authority. He had to include many Communists in the government of Czechoslovakia, which became again briefly a free, democratic (though in a somewhat curtailed form) country, until the Communist takeover of 1948.

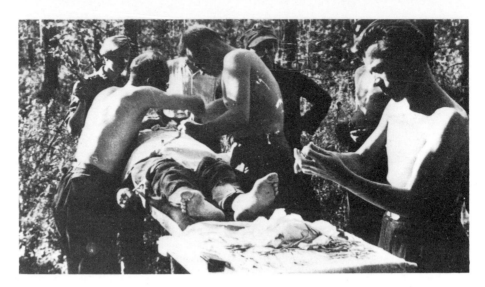

Above: A first-aid post in the open air for partisans in the Polish forests.

Below: Wounded partisans rounded up by the Germans and later hanged.

Poland

No COUNTRY in the Second World War suffered worse than Poland, not even Germany or Japan.

Poland was precariously positioned between two great powers, Germany and Russia, a thoroughly uncomfortable position, as grim events would prove. In the 1930s Poland vigorously avoided being drawn towards either of the threatening giants on either side, a policy which succeeded as long as the giants remained on unfriendly terms with each other. As Hitler hated Communism even more than the Polish leaders hated it, the policy seemed a reasonably safe one, especially when, in 1939, a firm British alliance was secured by the Poles. But in August 1939, Ribbentrop suddenly flew to Moscow and signed a non-aggression pact with the Soviet government. The giants had, temporarily, made a bargain, a bargain which included a carve-up of north-east Europe between them, a bargain which spelled doom for Poland. For with Russia neutralized, Hitler could safely pursue those territorial ambitions, including the reclamation of Danzig, which could only be satisfied at Poland's expense. It was true that Britain and France were bound to assist the Poles if they were attacked. But Hitler reasoned that they were unlikely to do so. They had not defended Czechoslovakia, so why should they defend Poland? On this point, Hitler miscalculated; but probably he was not greatly concerned with the danger of war with the Western democracies. France could easily be defeated, he considered. Britain would be harder to conquer, but Britain could do little to help Poland.

The invasion of Poland was not long delayed. Hitler initially ordered it for 25 August 1939, the day after publication of the Nazi-Soviet Pact, but he cancelled the order at the last moment (too late to stop one unit, which was annihilated by the Poles). Whatever the reason for this postponement, it was a short one. On 1 September, the German forces swept across the Polish frontier from north, south and west.

The invasion was precipitated by what appeared to be a Polish attack on a German radio station at Gleiwitz. Bullet-ridden bodies in Polish uniforms were displayed. In fact, these were the corpses of German prisoners, taken from a concentration camp, dressed in Polish uniforms and murdered. The incident was arranged by an SS expert in dirty tricks named Naujocks, who appears again in the story of the Netherlands.

British military authorities had estimated that Poland's 40 divisions might withstand the Germans for two weeks. It took less than three. On 17 September the Russians invaded from the east and independent Poland ceased to exist. It was partitioned (a familiar experience for the Poles) into three, the western part being incorporated into Germany, the eastern part into the Soviet Union, and a central section, which included Warsaw and Cracow, under German occupation.

In the weird and grisly conception of the Nazis, the Poles were an inferior race; moreover, Poland contained a very large proportion of Jews. The Nazi terror was therefore more ferocious in Poland than in other occupied countries. Between 1941 and 1945, over 3,000,000 people were exterminated in Auschwitz and nearby concentration camps. The Russians did not object to Poles or Jews on racial grounds, but were hardly less ferocious than the Germans in their pursuit of those who belonged to the social classes opposed to Communism. In short, the fate of Poland in 1939-45 was frightful, almost beyond comprehension. Events were complicated by the presence of two enemies instead of one and by the disastrous failure of the Poles to achieve unity among themselves. But this book is not about politics, and in spite–or because–of the special difficulties in Poland, resistance to German occupation was strong and widespread among virtually the whole population. Guerrilla warfare on a really large scale did not occur except during 1944, and since German reprisals were especially savage against the Poles, the resistance leaders had to make some cruel calculations before authorizing sabotage operations.

Polish intelligence was extremely efficient, and was responsible for one of the major espionage coups of the war. We have only recently become aware, as the result of a relaxation in security restrictions, of the tremendous importance to the Allied side of the source of secret information known in Britain as 'Ultra'. Shortly before the war began, the Poles had got hold of, or managed to make a copy of, an Enigma cipher machine which the Germans used throughout the war for their most secret communications. The Poles made a present of an Enigma machine to both the French and the British at the end of July 1939, and as a result the Allies were often able to read commands issued from Berlin as soon as their intended recipients.

Almost as valuable to London was the Polish underground's effort to discover the facts about the new rocket weapons developed by the Germans in the later stages of the war. Tips from Polish resistance, plus expert photo-interpretation in Britain, led to the RAF raid on the rocket-base of Peenemunde in August 1943 which virtually destroyed it. The Germans built a new range at Blizna, in a remote forest region in the south, out of reach of British bombers. Reports were soon being received by the

Poles of a new railway line in this region, and of the movement of large cigar-shaped objects covered by tarpaulin sheets. Villages in the neighbourhood were forcibly evacuated and a tight security fence set up. It was obvious that some kind of aerial torpedo was being tested. A number of sightings were reported, and it soon appeared that these missiles tended to land in a particular region, near the River Bug, where some civilian casualties occurred. Whenever a missile exploded, a German patrol would hurry to the scene, and all debris would be carefully collected.

This was a challenge to the Polish partisans. Though they lacked motor cars and motor bicycles, they organized their own patrols on foot. Several times they beat the Germans to the scene of the explosion, hastily collected bits of metal, and vanished. A technical committee in Warsaw examined the fragments and radioed its reports to London.

The results, however, were inconclusive. With London pressing for more information, plans were considered for capturing a missile intact. An attack on the rocket base itself had to be ruled out: it was too strongly defended. A slightly more hopeful alternative was to raid the train transporting the missile to the range. This would probably have been done—inevitably with high casualties and doubtful success—but for a lucky accident.

On 20 May 1944, a V2 landed near the Bug and failed to explode. Partisans reached it first, and managed to hide it by sinking it in a nearby stream. When the Germans arrived minutes later, the missile had disappeared and, after much angry stamping about in the boggy ground, they abandoned the search. Several days passed while things quietened down. Then, by night, the partisans came with two carts tied together and drawn by three horses. With great effort, the rocket was dragged from the stream, loaded on to the cart, and taken to a barn in a village nearby, where partisans mounted an unobtrusive 24-hour guard until technical experts from Warsaw arrived to take the missile to pieces, making notes and photographing every piece as they worked. As it had 25,000 parts, this was not a simple job.

A major problem remained: how to transfer all the information gained to London? It was eventually decided to send in person the expert, code-named 'Raphael' (Jerzy Chmielewski), who was in charge of the examination, together with written reports, photographs, and even some parts of the missile itself.

There was of course never any question of surreptitious aircraft landings in occupied Poland on the scale of those in France. The distance was so great that long-distance bombers from England could barely make it, and the shift of operations to Brindisi, in the heel of Italy, at the end of 1943 only knocked about 150 km off the distance. Moreover, so thick were the Germans on the ground that it was almost impossible to find a safe landing place anywhere in the country. Nevertheless, landings had taken place—two of them, to be exact. The aeroplane used was that old faithful, then comparatively new, the Dakota, specially modified with extra fuel tanks. The first flight took off from Brindisi, with a British crew, in April 1944. It landed safely at a prepared spot near Lublin, took off again with some difficulty because of tall trees, and returned to Brindisi. A second flight at the end of May used an abandoned German airfield about 70 km east of Cracow. It too was a success, spending only six minutes on the ground while it exchanged passengers, and returned to Brindisi without incident.

The third flight, on which 'Raphael' was to leave Poland with his valuable information, was scheduled for 25 July. It would have taken place sooner but for adverse weather conditions and the difficulty of finding another landing place. In the end, despite the obvious risk, it was decided to use the same deserted airfield in the Cracow region. At 8 pm on the agreed date, the Dakota took off from Brindisi and headed north.

Unknown to crew or passengers, the flight was almost called off at the last moment. To the consternation of the reception committee, a party of Germans had turned up unexpectedly at the airfield, and shortly afterwards a pair of German reconnaissance aircraft landed there. It looked as if the place was being reactivated, and at a most inconvenient moment. The Poles waited anxiously and were just about to send a signal cancelling the Dakota flight when the reconnaissance aircraft took off again and the Germans packed up and left.

The airfield was as deserted as before, but there was another problem worrying the Poles. It had been raining heavily for some time and the ground had become soft. It was really not fit for use. Nevertheless, after some argument, the go-ahead was signalled.

Soon after midnight, the silence of the darkened countryside was shattered by the roar of the approaching aircraft. Powerful lights flashed downwards as the Dakota roared overhead, awakening every German, the anxious spectators must have thought, between them and Berlin. It landed safely. The arriving passengers climbed out and swiftly vanished into the night; the departing passengers took their places. The engines roared, the flaps wagged, but the plane remained where she was, the wheels deep in the soft ground. The Polish captain of the flight (in accordance with Polish Air Force practice, he was the navigator, not the pilot) ordered everyone off, but after inspecting the wheels he and the crew decided that the position was hopeless. The flight would have to be abandoned and the plane burned where she stood. But first, the local people tried digging out the wheels and cramming straw underneath them. Everyone got back on board, and the engines roared again as the plane tried to pick herself out of the mud. But she did not budge. Once again, everyone clambered out, and the crew were preparing to throw petrol over the plane when the officer in charge of the reception committee suggested putting planks under the wheels. For the third time the plane loaded up, and the pilot opened the throttle. Slowly she began to move, then accelerated and, drowning the cheers of those left

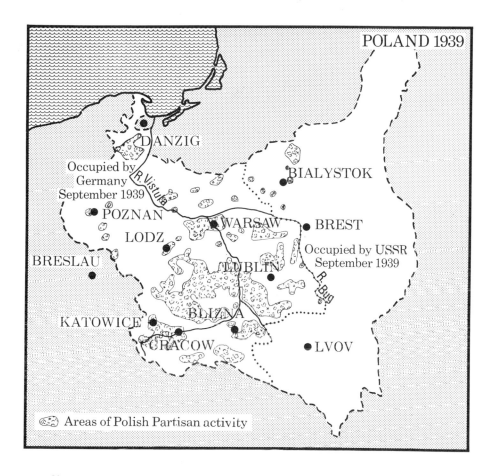

POLAND 1939

Occupied by Germany September 1939

Occupied by USSR September 1939

R. Vistula

R. Bug

DANZIG
BIALYSTOK
POZNAN
WARSAW
BREST
LODZ
BRESLAU
LUBLIN
BLIZNA
KATOWICE
CRACOW
LVOV

🐾 Areas of Polish Partisan activity

standing on the field, roared upwards into the sky. She had been on the ground one hour and ten minutes, which was one hour and five minutes longer than the captain had planned on, but had got away with it.

She reached Brindisi before 6 am and two days later 'Raphael' and his bag of V2 parts were in London. Thus, although it is impossible to say what effect this whole enterprise had in defending London from the V2, the authorities knew virtually all there was to know about Hitler's new secret weapon a clear two months before the first one was launched.

The Polish 'Home Army', which was to fight one of the most heroic and hopeless battles of the war, was formed before the end of 1939. It was a centrally organized resistance movement loyal to the exiled Polish government, which settled in London after the fall of France with General Sikorsky as both prime minister and commander-in-chief. The Home Army (it was not actually known by that name until 1942) was supported by the bulk of the Polish people and the main political parties though not by the Communists, nor by an extreme right-wing, nationalist group.

The Home Army at its height numbered about 400,000 men, including full-time partisan units living in the forests (some even wearing uniform), plus a small full-time staff living completely underground. The remainder were part-time soldiers, performing a regular job during the day and undertaking Home Army duty at other times.

A major problem for the Home Army was the acquisition of arms. Some were retained after the surrender and hidden, often buried. Of these weapons, some were discovered by the Germans, some deteriorated and became useless, and some were for one reason or another inaccessible when the crisis came and they were wanted quickly. Some arms were parachuted in by the RAF, but such flights were rare. In 1940, Poland was only just within range of British aircraft. Nor had this situation improved much by August 1944, when Warsaw rose against the Germans. Some weapons were manufactured, and some were stolen or captured from the Germans, but that was hardly a reliable source of supply. At the time of the Warsaw Rising, perhaps as many as nine out of ten soldiers in the Home Army were virtually unarmed, and there was a total absence of heavy weapons, artillery, tanks, etc. The arms problem was never solved.

The immediate task of the Home Army was to unite the defeated country and to organize resistance to the Germans. As the representative of the exiled government in London, it looked forward to a time when the Germans would be defeated and it could rise to reclaim the country for the rightful government–i.e. the government in London. This role became especially important when it became apparent that the Germans would be driven from Poland by Russian, not British or American forces.

A good deal of sabotage was carried out from 1940 onwards by units of the Home Army. The railways were an obvious target, and the Poles used a trick similar to one adopted by French saboteurs, adding an abrasive or corrosive substance to the grease in the grease box. This made the engine seize up some time later but–this was important in view of the German willingness to exact vicious reprisals–no cause for the breakdown was obvious and sabotage could not be proved. During the period between the German-Soviet Pact and the German attack on Russia, Stalin kindly supplied his brother-dictator with raw materials on a vast scale, and most of this traffic passed through Poland. The Poles blew up trains using a delayed-timing device which made it difficult for the Germans to know where the bomb had been attached.

In 1941, following the German attack on Russia, diplomatic relations between Poland and the Soviet Union were restored, and an agreement was signed by Moscow and the Polish government in exile. This had several favourable results. It meant that the Poles held in Russian prisons and camps since the Soviet takeover of east Poland in September 1939 were released. A Polish army was created in Russia under General Anders, himself formerly a prisoner of the Russians.

One rather important topic was not discussed at this time: the eastern frontier of Poland. The Russians had been driven out of eastern Poland, which they called Western Belorussia and the Western Ukraine, in 1941.

So far as the Poles were concerned, Russian territory began at the pre-1939 frontier, but the Russians, while admitting that their agreement with Hitler was now indisputably defunct, were making no admissions on this question. Anyone who had time to think very far ahead could foresee trouble here.

Since Stalin had executed most of the senior officers in the political purges of the late 1930s, the Red Army did not put up much resistance to the Germans, whose advance was at first extremely rapid. The Poles supplied much intelligence information direct to the Russians, but it was of little assistance: knowing what the enemy is going to do does not necessarily mean that you can stop him doing it. 'Diversionary activities' (i.e. for the most part, sabotage) were also carried on in the German rear, and even on Russian territory, by Home Army men in the forced-labour gangs following the troops' advance. There were some clashes between Polish and Soviet guerrilla groups, though there was also some co-operation.

The Poles displayed great ingenuity in manufacturing the tools of sabotage. They invented, for example, a small bomb in the form of a harmless-looking cylinder which could be slipped into the tail assembly of an aircraft. It was set off at a certain height by changes in atmospheric pressure, and is said to have accounted for the destruction of 18 Luftwaffe aeroplanes. A type of hand grenade which was to prove effective, in certain circumstances, against tanks was made from plastic cups, of which the Home Army procured 10,000, and another type was made from the fuel container of a common make of paraffin lamp. Some weapons were made in secret workshops, others comparatively openly in factories under some kind of cover. One factory was making fire-extinguishers, which the Germans knew and approved, but it was also turning out flame-throwers, which the Germans did not know and would not have approved. Nor did they object when the Poles tested their flame-throwers in the middle of Warsaw: they had taken the trouble to inform the German police that they were experimenting with a new type of fire extinguisher, and some flames and smoke might result from the experiments.

In spite of these successes, more valuable psychologically than militarily, it was a grim existence for the inhabitants of Poland. For Jews, it was worse than grim.

The Nazis at first crammed all Jews into ghettoes in cities, the largest being the Warsaw ghetto. Among other forms of persecution, they restricted them to food rations so low that they would all have starved slowly to death but for assistance from outside. Nevertheless, conditions inside the ghettoes were appalling, with corpses lying in the street and buildings crammed with increasingly skeletal people. Early in 1942, rumours of the mass extermination of Jews were circulating, at first disbelieved by most people, but eventually proved true in Warsaw by simple observation: the camp to which the Jews were being taken was

Above: Executions of Polish civilians, such as these in Silesia, were carried on indiscriminately.

Opposite top: A patrol of the underground army in camouflage uniform in SE Poland in January 1944.

Opposite centre: A PIAT anti-tank gun, dropped by a British plane, in use during the Warsaw Rising.

Below: The Polish army leaders Moczar (centre) and Kunicki (right) with the Soviet commander Jakovlev in Lublin province.

nowhere near big enough to absorb the numbers of people who had entered it – and had not come out. Later, the Home Army extracted a sample from three railway-carriage loads of human hair, in a train from Treblinka. Chemical analysis showed that the Jews – 200,000 had already gone from the Warsaw ghetto – had been killed by a gas containing hydrogen cyanide.

Late in 1942, the remaining Jews in the ghetto decided on militant resistance. The Home Army provided some guns, ammunition and other aid. The Jews also managed to buy some arms from Germans, and in January 1943, when the SS entered the ghetto to round up more victims, they were met with gunfire. In April, the Germans decided to annihilate the ghetto. They used artillery and incendiaries, against which rifles and home-made grenades were not effective. Nevertheless, the Jews managed to kill about 100 Germans and to destroy factories engaged in war production for Germany. By the end of May the ghetto, or what was left of it, was empty. About 100 Jews had escaped through the sewers with the aid of Home Army units. The rest, over 400,000, had either died in the fighting or were about to die in the death camps to which they had been taken. (In Warsaw, remarked General Bor-Komorowski, one never came across the 'good' Germans he had since been told about.)

Many remarkable deeds were performed in the field by Polish partisans, a few of whom survived to tell their stories. Among the majority who did not was the officer known as *Ponury* ('Gloomy'), Lieutenant Jan Piwnik, whose code name was perhaps derived from his rather grim expression, accentuated by the dark band of eyebrow running unbroken across his face.

Soon after parachuting into Poland in 1942, 'Ponury' was appointed to command a unit in the east. He was quickly captured by the Germans, but escaped and returned to Warsaw. About the same time, another four-man partisan group who had carried out a successful series of sabotage acts, was arrested near Pinsk. One died under interrogation, the other three were imprisoned in Pinsk, and 'Ponury' was given the job of getting them out. He was told he could have anything the Home Army could provide, and he formed a formidable strike group of about sixteen men, with a car and two lorries. There was also – invaluably – a contact at the prison, a Home Army man employed as a guard. 'Ponury' found himself a hideaway in Pinsk, and began to gather information and consider tactics. Bribery had to be ruled out. An actual raid was the only way.

After careful planning, the raid was set for 5 pm, 18 January. An Opel car drew up at the prison gates and a man leaned out, demanding in an angry voice that the gates should be opened. As he spoke German and was wearing an SS uniform, the guard instinctively obeyed, and the car shot through. The guard, suddenly suspicious, reached for his rifle but was struck down. At the inner gate, the same trick worked again. A foot patrol followed the car into the prison while two other groups scaled the walls with ladders. One of them reached the office of the prison commander and, after a few bursts of submaghine-gun fire, the keys of the prison were acquired. The keys opened the last obstacle between 'Ponury's' party in the Opel and the centre of the prison, and within two or three minutes all three groups were united inside. 'Ponury' himself raced to unlock the cells, and released about fifty men, including several Soviet partisans and, of course, the three men he had come for. The car disappeared into the night, while the main body of the attackers leaped into the waiting lorry, which roared off in another direction, scattering barbs in the road behind it to pierce the tyres of any pursuing vehicle.

A few weeks later, 'Ponury' left Warsaw again, this time heading for the wooded country to the south where he was born, as the leader of a group of partisans, including two of his comrades from the Pinsk escape. He proved to be an ideal forest guerrilla leader, his only serious fault being his disinclination to obey orders he did not like. He was operating in an area where the local population could be depended on for support and where the extensive forests gave ample cover. As a result of reorganization among other units, he had a large force under his command, some 300 men in arms, with more available if weapons could be found. During subsequent operations, some German arms were captured, and 'Ponury's' force, which he divided into three separate groups, expanded. He was able to mount large-scale attacks with comparative impunity, but this had the unfortunate result that the local people suffered horribly from German reprisals. In retaliation for 'Ponury's' raid on the Warsaw-Cracow express (from which he obtained a rich haul in weapons and money) the Germans razed a whole village, murdering most of the 200 inhabitants.

In July 1943 the Germans mounted a large-scale operation, with some 4,000 troops, to root out and destroy 'Ponury' and his men. Warned of their approach, 'Ponury' fell back before them and, after a series of exhausting marches, at the end of which his men could barely stand up for exhaustion and hunger, he shook the Germans off. Soon afterwards, he was ordered to desist from his guerrilla activities because of the heavy cost in reprisals, but after a time he returned to his men, apparently against orders. He was soon on the retreat again as the Germans began a second operation to wipe him out, but once again, he gave them the slip. The Germans did find his main base, which was in a remote, hilly district, and destroyed it.

It seemed obvious that a traitor was at work: the Germans could hardly have located the partisans' camp without inside information. But no one could have been more shocked than 'Ponury' when it was revealed that the traitor was none other than 'Motor', a young officer who had shared the back seat of the Opel with him at Pinsk and been one of his closest comrades ever since. 'Motor' was later executed by his own people. It seems that the Gestapo had his mother in custody and blackmailed him into treachery.

Meanwhile, 'Ponury' had been relieved of his command by his superiors, who had brought the insubordinate guerrilla leader to heel by withholding supplies from his partisans. Later he returned to the forests and the marshes. He was killed in action against the Germans, 15 June 1944.

The spring and summer of 1943 was a disastrous period for the Poles. In April, the advancing Germans discovered the mass graves of Polish officers in the Forest of Katyn. There was and is little doubt that these were some of the troops driven east by the German advance in 1939, who had fallen into Russian hands and not been heard of thereafter. The Russians denied responsibility, saying it was all a German propaganda trick. The Poles in London joined in a demand that the International Red Cross should investigate the incident. The Soviet government peremptorily refused the Red Cross access and broke off diplomatic relations with the Poles.

The Polish government in exile has been blamed by historians for provoking this disastrous breach with Russia by its demand for an unbiased investigation of the Katyn massacre. But they would have to have been remarkably hard-headed realists to sit tight and ignore the revelation that the cream of their country's young men had been massacred by foreigners with whom at the time they were not even at war.

Two months later, more blows fell. The Germans by some means not established suddenly learned a lot more about the leaders of the underground in Warsaw than they had known before. They rounded up many of them including – a real disaster – the commander of the Home Army, General Grot-Rowecki. (He was sent to Germany and shot during the Warsaw Rising over a year later on Hitler's orders.) A few days after Grot-Rowecki's arrest came the news of the flying accident at Gibraltar in which General Sikorski was killed.

The replacements for these two Polish leaders were not, could not be, of comparable stature. The deputy commander of the Home Army, who stepped up to take over from Grot-Rowecki, was General Bor-Komorowski ('Bor' was his wartime code-name). He was an aristocratic former cavalry commander, gallant, honourable, conservative. He had little experience of command and he was far from being the ideal character for leading a national resistance movement. He was certainly not the man likely to be able to establish rapport with the Communists, and neither was the new (London-based) commander-in-chief, General Sosnkowski, who was associated with the prewar, right-wing regime. However, Sosnkowski did not see eye to eye with the new premier (there was no one who could have taken both jobs, like Sikorski) of the government in exile, Mikolajczyk.

All three men were Polish patriots and all were able men, but it can hardly be denied that the changes at the top forced upon the Poles by the events of that cruel week at the end of June led to a weakening in leadership. But it seems presumptuous to criticize men working under the conditions of German-occupied Poland, where Bor-Komorowski, and many others, lived in secret, without a break, for five years. In his book *The*

Secret Army (London 1950) he tells how the strain of living in constant fear of arrest affected one of the Polish resistance leaders.

This was Colonel M. Drobnik, code-named 'Woodpecker', who was chief of the Home Army's intelligence and a man most urgently wanted by the Gestapo. At a high-level staff meeting in a private house, attended by 'Woodpecker', a loud knocking was suddenly heard at the front door. Probably everyone present immediately assumed it was the Gestapo, and cursed the bad luck that had led them to this particular meeting house as, unlike most of their other meeting places, it was not provided with any means of escape in the event of a raid. 'Woodpecker', unnoticed, slipped from the room, while the others sat frozen until the owner of the house put her head round the door and reassured them. It was merely a man come to read the electric meter, a bad-tempered fellow, it would seem, and in a hurry. Sighs of relief. The officers turned back to the table and, just as they noticed that 'Woodpecker's' chair was empty, he staggered back into the room on the point of collapse. Knowing that the Gestapo were on his trail, and indeed almost certain to catch up with him soon, he had taken poison, which he carried in a glass phial, to make certain that the Gestapo would not get the chance to make him talk.

'Woodpecker' did not die, although he lay at death's door for a fortnight. Within a few days of his release from hospital, the Gestapo did arrest him. He was no longer carrying poison, but withstood torture and said nothing. He was then shot.

As the tide turned slowly against Germany, the Home Army stepped up its campaign. Operation *Burza* ('Tempest') went into effect early in 1944, when the Germans were in retreat after their defeats in Russia the previous year. It was not entirely clear what *Burza* entailed. It was certainly not a rising, rather an intensification of 'diversionary activities', sabotage, etc., but there was some disagreement over its extent and location. By staging partisan attacks in the countryside, it was hoped to avoid severe reprisals, but some, such as General Okulicki, who was parachuted into Poland in May and was to become Bor-Komorowski's successor as commander of the Home Army, favoured action in the cities also. A full-scale rising was out of the question as long as the Germans retained good order, but Okulicki reasoned that the Germans would be bound to defend Warsaw from the Russians and that a rising in the city timed to coincide with the Russian attack would hasten the German defeat and restrict the destruction and loss of civilian life. There was another argument in favour of a rising which was not so much military as political in character. If the Poles were able to regain possession of their capital themselves, and set up at least a skeletal administration, they would be in a position to receive the Russians as hosts, and it would be difficult for the Communists to enforce their own authority. It was this consideration that weighed most heavily with Home Army leaders and with the Polish government in London. General Sosnkowski, it is true, was extremely doubtful about a rising in Warsaw, but he never came down firmly against it and during the vital period immediately before the rising began, he was away from London.

The Russians had already shown that they regarded eastern Poland as Soviet territory. Their advance forces co-operated amiably with Polish partisans but after a time, when the NKVD (secret police) joined the front-line troops, attitudes changed. Polish partisans were compelled to disarm, were forcibly enrolled in Soviet-controlled units, or were shot.

The conflict over the eastern frontier certainly made it harder to reach any agreement with the Russians. In London, Churchill pressed the Poles to make at least some concessions in the east, but Mikolajczyk was adamant. He dared not cede an inch of territory for fear of antagonizing his own people. Thus the Poles overplayed their hand in 1944 as they had in 1939. Some form of co-operation with the Russians was a pre-requisite of a general revolt in Warsaw, but as long as the Poles refused to budge on the frontier question, agreement was impossible. Some less formal arrangement might have been made locally, but Bor-Komorowski and his staff were as suspicious of the Russians (not without reason) as their superiors in London. Bor-Komorowski did make several attempts to initiate military co-operation with the Soviet commanders, but received no reply to his perhaps rather half-hearted enquiries.

As the Warsaw Rising was to turn into such a frightful disaster, the events leading up to it, the causes and responsibility for it, have been the subject of much discussion (see, for instance, Jan Ciechanowski, *The Warsaw Rising of 1944*, Cambridge 1974). There is not space to enter into the discussion here, but the events immediately preceding the Rising must be briefly outlined.

On 25 July, Bor-Komorowski signalled London. 'We are ready to fight for Warsaw at any moment...' Two weeks earlier, he had discounted such an event, but he had changed his mind under pressure from Okulicki and those who agreed with him and in view of what he regarded as signs of German collapse. The assassination attempt on Hitler, on 20 July, helped to convince Bor that the Reich was disintegrating, and three days later a panic flight from Warsaw by German civilians confirmed that impression. The Russian advance had been remarkably fast, and on the day Bor sent his message there was reason to think that they would be in Warsaw in hardly more than a week. It was reckoned that the Home Army in Warsaw could take the offensive against the Germans for two or three days, and after that they could hold out for about a week in a defensive posture before their shortage of arms and ammunition became serious. The timing of the rising therefore had to be calculated with some care; the margin of error was small.

In his 25 July message, Bor had also asked for the Polish Parachute Brigade to be dropped on Warsaw and for German airfields nearby to be

50

bombed. These were not vital conditions, but Warsaw was being extremely optimistic in even suggesting that they might be fulfilled. There was not the slightest hope of it: the only aircraft capable of transporting the British-based Parachute Brigade was the Liberator, and 265 of them would have been required – less than two months after the Normandy invasion! Indeed, it was far from certain that the Allies would be able to provide any airborne help at all, because of the great distances involved, unless the Russians allowed them to use their air bases. This the Russians were not prepared to do.

While the difficult task of secretly mobilizing an army of close to 40,000 men in an occupied city was set in motion, Bor-Komorowski and his closest colleagues had to decide the moment for the rising to start. Opinions were divided. 'Monter' (Colonel Chrusciel), Home Army commander of the Warsaw area, gave a rather depressing account of the weapons available to his forces – almost exclusively light weapons, and not many of them. Nevertheless, he thought he could hold out, even without Russian help, for a fortnight if necessary.

By 27 July, it was apparent to the Poles in Warsaw that the Germans had recovered from their panic of a few days earlier. They knew also that the divisions resisting the Russians had been reinforced, and they were worried by signs that the Germans might forcibly evacuate the population of Warsaw, which would put paid to an attempted rising Meanwhile, news came in of another Home Army unit disbanded by the Russians. Altogether, the situation was extremely complicated and the tension severe. On psychological grounds alone, it might have been impossible for the Home Army command to cancel the rising.

On 28 July the decision was taken to start the rising when the Soviet troops reached Praga, the 'East End' of Warsaw, on the other side of the Vistula. At this time, the Russians themselves expected to be in Praga on 6 August. Already, the sound of Russian artillery could be heard, and Soviet aircraft flew over the city. To the Poles in Warsaw, it seemed that their moment had come, though in fact the Soviets were about to become engaged in a major battle which checked their advance. By 1 August, the Germans, temporarily, were in command. But the Warsaw Rising had begun.

At the usual afternoon briefing on 31 July, two things had happened. First, news had come that the Polish prime minister, Mikolajczyk, was in Moscow conferring with Stalin. This was very good news, as it seemed to presage the restoration of diplomatic relations and probably Russian assistance to the Poles in Warsaw; in fact, Mikolajczyk got nowhere with Stalin. The second surprise was the belated arrival of 'Monter' at the meeting with the momentous news that Russian tanks were in Praga. He insisted that the rising should begin at once, otherwise it would be too late and the Russians would take over. On this, Bor-Komorowski, having gained the assent of the delegate of the London-based government, gave

Top: An exhausted member of the underground army being helped out of the sewers during the Warsaw Rising.

Above: Members of the Jewish Fighters' Association in action in the Ghetto Rising of April 1943.

Opposite: The centre and Old Town of Warsaw were almost entirely destroyed during the Rising.

the order to begin the Rising at 5 pm on the next day.

Unfortunately, 'Monter's' report had been incorrect. There were no Russian tanks in Praga. They were some miles farther off, and they were not coming any nearer.

Whether the abrupt cessation of the Russian advance in Poland was due to German pressure or to Stalin's desire to see his opponents in Warsaw wiped out by the Germans is a matter for argument. Certainly the Russians made little effort to help the Rising, and without Russian help the Rising was doomed. Bor-Komorowski remarked how very different things would have been if the armies at Warsaw's gates had been American and British. The RAF made a few supply-dropping sorties, but casualties were shockingly high and Air Marshal Slessor felt compelled to forbid further flights, though the order was later overruled. The Russians also dropped some weapons and food, when it was already too late, and as they did not use parachutes, much of what they dropped was ruined. Too late also they at last permitted use of their airfields for American planes to refuel, and a vast fleet of B17s made a massive high-level drop on 18 September. Unfortunately, most of the parachutes fell outside the territory, by that time very small, held by the Poles, and a planned second flight never took place because Warsaw surrendered first.

The Poles therefore mounted their rising without first making sure of either substantial help from the Allies or co-operation with the Russians. One, perhaps both, of these conditions was imperative if the hopelessly outnumbered and outgunned partisans were not to be swiftly annihilated.

Nevertheless, for a people crushed under the Nazi heel for five long years, the first few days of August 1944 were an exhilarating time. Within three hours of the beginning of the rising (though in some parts of the city, inevitably, it began ahead of schedule), the Polish flag could be seen flying from the top of the highest building in Warsaw, and before darkness combined with the smoke of battle to obliterate the scene, more flags had appeared on the city hall, the post office, and other major buildings. The Germans had been taken by surprise. It was some time before tanks appeared on the streets, and they were not at first particularly effective. A bottle of petrol corked with explosive proved quite effective and home-made grenades, tied in bunches and thrown under a caterpillar track, could disable a tank. Several were captured and though most of them had been rendered immobile their guns could still be used; they were more powerful than any weapon the Poles possessed. About two-thirds of the city on the west bank of the Vistula was in Polish hands on the second day of the rising, though there were pockets of Germans within the Polish areas.

There were many heroic and many horrid incidents. The Germans took to using civilians as cover for their troops. At one place they advanced up a street behind a ladder to which Polish citizens had been tied. It was a cruel decision for the local Home Army commander. Eventually he gave the order to fire, killing both Germans and Poles. As he said, if he had not fired, all the Germans in Warsaw would have adopted such tactics. In another part of the city, a twelve-year-old boy with a petrol bomb captured a Tiger tank single-handed.

Indeed, the whole city joined the fight. It was not just the Home Army that sprang from the doors and cellars to attack the enemy; practically every man, woman and child in Warsaw was anxious to help, including the Communists. But on 4 August, the reassuring sound of the Russian guns across the Vistula could no longer be heard. If the Poles had known they were not be heard again for five weeks, they might as well have surrendered then. The Poles made no major conquests after the first two or three days of fighting – one or two major buildings had been recaptured by the Germans – and among the commanders, an uncomfortable apprehension that the Russians might not arrive as fast as they had assumed began to be felt. Soviet aeroplanes had disappeared from the sky and the Luftwaffe was back. A force of Junker bombers attacked the district of Wola, where Home Army headquarters were located. General Bor found it necessary to issue an urgent warning about wasting ammunition, and reluctantly, the Home Army had to go over to defence. One encouraging sign was the appearance of two Halifaxes over Warsaw. The partisans picked up their parachuted stores, but what no one in Warsaw realised was that those two aircraft were the only ones to fulfil a mission on which fourteen had set out.

The Poles had some ingenious tricks which at least held up the Germans even if they did not do them any damage. Certain places were marked 'Beware of Mines!' which kept the Tigers away although there were no mines present. One group managed to frighten off advancing tanks by rolling barrels down a slope towards them; the tank crews were not taking any chances with the contents, though in fact the barrels were empty. A simple clothes line with bottles attached, strung across a street, looked sinister enough to make another tank retreat.

Such tactics might have proved useful had help been on the way. But you cannot frighten off tanks with empty bottles for long.

Home Army headquarters were located in a factory in a western district of the city, Wola, where the Germans began a push to establish an east-west link with the river. They drove in wedges, attacking street by street, first with bombs and incendiaries, then with tanks and infantry carrying flame-throwers and grenades. The barricades began to crumble, and on 7 August headquarters had to be moved to the Old Town. The staff officers dodged across the desolation that had been the Jewish Ghetto between bursts of machine-gun fire. German sharp-shooters, well placed to stop them in a high church tower, were eliminated when the tower was blasted by one of the captured tanks.

The area held by the Home Army was shrinking day by day, not contracting evenly upon a centre, but splitting into small areas, most of them out of touch with the others. German fire-power was building up steadily, with air raids every hour, armoured trains carrying heavy guns and mortars, and miniature robot tanks, crammed with explosive, which were controlled from orthodox tanks and sent to blow up barricades. German reinforcements arrived from the west, and a new SS commander took over, von dem Bach-Zelewski, who had a reputation as an effective repressor of revolts. The Germans had plenty of ammunition, but the Poles were desperately short, not only of ammunition, but of every kind of supplies, including food. Renewed drops by the RAF and South African Air Force brought only a temporary respite. Yet they did enable the Home Army to mount several new attacks. After a long siege, in which the German garrison was reduced to a drop of soup each per day, the central telephone building fell to the Poles in a bloody floor-by-floor fight. Equally ferocious was the struggle for German police headquarters, in which the decisive battle took place in a church. Between pillars and pews, German and Pole exchanged submachine-gun fire and hurled grenades at 10 metres range. Finally, the church was burned out, though the pillar in which the heart of Frederick Chopin was immured remained untouched.

On 19 August, the Germans began to move in on the Old Town of Warsaw in overwhelming force. Among their artillery was a 600 mm battery—a sledgehammer, one might think, to crack a nut (though a very tough nut). The old houses collapsed into heaps of rubble, often burying dozens of people, beyond hope of rescue, in the cellars (people soon learned that the safest shelter was in buildings already ruined). The air was so thick with dust and smoke that it was hard to see across a street. The noise was shattering, and bursts of flames sprang up here and there: the old carved beams burned particularly well. The Poles had to fight fires as desperately as they were fighting Germans. Slowly and surely, the Old Town, an area little more than half a mile square, was reduced to rubble. The main buildings were often taken by the Germans during the day and retaken by the Poles during the night, when the artillery ceased, but increasingly such fights were merely for possession of a smoking ruin.

Great efforts had been made to establish contact between the Old Town and the district of Zoliborz, to the north, separated by German-held territory. A message was once carried across by a young boy leading his goat but when he attempted to repeat the journey next day he did not arrive at his destination. Then two men got through from Zoliborz. They arrived at Home Army HQ black from the waist down with foul-smelling slime. They had come through the sewers.

As the situation grew worse, the sewers were used more and more for communication and even transport of food and supplies. The sewers had been used to get in and out of the Ghetto, but they had been neglected since. They were valuable lifelines, in a sense, but they were also places of horror. However ghastly conditions were above ground, they were preferable to the conditions below.

For a start, the sewers were dark–pitch black in fact, the kind of darkness only experienced underground when the human eye is no more use than a stone. Artificial lights were, in general, too risky. Built in the 19th century, the Warsaw sewers formed a complex network of tunnels below the streets. The tunnels were seldom high enough for a man to stand upright, and many that were in daily use during the Rising were only one metre from top to bottom. As they were rounded, the floor was never level, and the bottom was littered with all kinds of rubbish, some of it sharp. It was dangerous to use the hands to assist progress, because the smallest scratch in that environment meant blood-poisoning. The air was so foul that the eyes smarted and watered. The main routes through this hellish labyrinth were marked with a string, which nervous hands clasped for reassurance as well as guidance. To put up a hand and find the string not there brought instant terror; for someone who lost the way in the sewers was as good as dead. Yet the routes had first to be worked out by volunteers. Several never reappeared from the tunnels they explored. Many of them were women–*Kanalarki* (sewer girls) as they were called.

Finally, the sewers were, of course, still performing the task for which they were built, and it was sometimes necessary to wade chest high through the flood. One slip of the foot was enough for the current to sweep its victim off his feet, to be drowned in the black tide.

Travel in these conditions was excruciatingly slow, especially when going against the current, which flowed west to east, towards the river. One sewer route from the beleaguered Old Town to the city centre, though no more than a mile long, took nine hours to negotiate. Some of the tunnels here were particularly narrow, and forward progress was made with the aid of short sticks held in each hand, in a series of cramped little hops like a crippled kangaroo. From such a journey, strong men emerged on the point of collapse.

For some time the Germans did not realise that a whole transport and communications system had come into existence under their feet. Once they had tumbled to it, they introduced new horrors to the nightmare world beneath the streets. They set up barricades and booby-traps–a grenade hanging from the roof of a tunnel which exploded when someone bumped into it, a barricade acting as a dam which, when removed, released a sudden flood to drown those in the tunnel. Sentries were posted at manholes and when they heard sounds, lobbed in a grenade or poured in petrol and set it ablaze. The Germans went into the sewers themselves, and grisly battles were fought in the blackness and stink. Hand-to-hand fights sometimes took place: two men trying to drown each other in human excrement, surely the nadir of civilization.

As the Old Town collapsed into rubble, Bor-Komorowski and his staff, including two political officials over sixty years old, had to take to the sewers to reach the city centre, where they hoped to hold out a little longer. The nine-hour route through three-foot-high tunnels was impossible for elderly men, and another had to be found. At first the alternative route seemed impassable, but by adjusting dams in other tunnels, the flow was reduced to knee height. On 26 August, Bor-Komorowski and his staff left what a month before had been a beautiful old city with medieval cathedral and churches and was now an almost unrecognizable pile of rubble. They descended a manhole in Krasinski Square, less than 200 metres from German machine guns, and emerged several hours later into a district where a pattern of streets still existed and buildings were still entered by doors, rather than a hole in a pile of bricks.

Although conditions were so much better in the city centre, the fall of the Old Town a few days later meant that the Germans would soon be attacking in greater force. On 4 September, a direct hit by a 600 mm shell destroyed the building where Home Army HQ were established, though the commander and high-ranking officers were absent at the time. The new HQ was located in a building within 300 metres of German positions: experience had shown that it was safer to be near the battle lines because the Germans did not direct their artillery at targets too close to their own men.

As the districts held by the Poles were, one by one, recaptured by the Germans, the refugee problem became acute. Massacres by German troops created panic among civilians already half-starved, dispossessed and wretched. Hospitals were over-crowded, there were many cases of dysentery and growing dangers of worse epidemics. From 2 September there was no bread. From 4 September there was no electricity, except what a few petrol-driven generators could provide. Ammunition was down to a dozen rounds per man. Besides the shortage of food – cats and dogs were already being killed for meat and pigeons were eagerly hunted – there was a scarcity of water. A few basement taps could be coaxed into a slow drip, but they were drying up. Nothing worked. The whole city was rapidly reverting to the state of a primeval jungle, but a jungle of burnt-out buildings, ripped-up pavements, ruptured gas-pipes and mountainous piles of rubble.

On 10 September terms for a Polish surrender were under discussion; but the Home Army commander was encouraged to delay by the reappearance over Warsaw of Soviet aircraft and the sound, not heard since the first few days of the Rising, of the Red Army's guns. New attempts were made to contact the Russians and procure assistance, but with only a limited response. Tinned food (American) and rifle ammunition was dropped, but much of the food was damaged and some of the ammunition did not fit any of the Poles' motley, but mostly German, assortment of small arms. Heavy weapons were dropped on succeeding nights, but again many were wrecked by impact with the ground. Attempts to contact the Soviet commander, Marshal Rokossovsky, either in person by groups crossing the Vistula, or by telephone, were unsuccessful. On the other hand, a

Soviet officer arrived by parachute saying he came from Rokossovsky; but he was apparently only instructed to report on the situation in the city, not to arrange co-operation. Soviet policy was, and is, often exceedingly mysterious, and must remain so as long as their records are closed, but probably a great deal that seems mysterious and sinister is to be explained by simple inefficiency, poor communication, etc. It is quite clear, however, that the Russians wanted nothing to do with the Home Army leaders or the representatives of the Polish government in exile, who were adumbrated in Soviet propaganda as war criminals. Once the Russians had taken Praga, there was nothing to stop them sending troops to reinforce the Poles. A few troops did cross the river, untrained Polish peasants according to Bor-Komorowski, more trouble than they were worth.

After the comparative failure of the giant American supply drop on 18 September, the dying city sank into hopelessness. The Russians showed no sign of advancing across the river, and their aeroplanes had again disappeared from the sky. On 23 September, the district held by the Home Army on the western bank of the Vistula, and therefore nearest to the Russians, was recaptured by the Germans: its defenders had not eaten anything for four days. A day or two later the district of Mokotow also fell, leaving the Poles in command of only two shrinking areas in the city. On 27 September Bor-Komorowski took the decision to cease resistance. There was no hope left. Terms were submitted to the German commander, von dem Bach-Zelewski, who promised that the Home Army men would be treated as regular soldiers. Although the Poles had no cause to put their trust in German promises, this one was kept. The surrender was signed on 2 October. The Germans, who were not winning many battles in 1944, had recaptured Warsaw.

General Bor-Komorowski was sent to Colditz and liberated in 1945. He died in England in 1966. He was succeeded as commander of the Home Army by General Okulicki, but after the surrender of Warsaw, resistance was over for the Poles and the Home Army was disbanded a few months later, during the successful Russian offensive of the winter. Okulicki and other top leaders of the Home Army were arrested—under a safe conduct—by the Russians and later imprisoned. Okulicki defended himself courageously at his trial in Moscow but was sentenced to ten years. He died in prison.

The Polish casualties during the Warsaw Rising totalled about 200,000, the vast majority of them civilians. In the ranks of the Home Army, about one-third died during the two months fighting and more than half the remainder were wounded. Practically the whole city of Warsaw was destroyed. No great city had suffered such thorough devastation since ancient times (though one or two others were soon to suffer almost as badly). The Rising, with all its horror and heroism, was fruitless, a disaster: the sole beneficiaries were the power politicians of the Kremlin.

Above: An angry encounter during the almost bloodless German invasion of Denmark in 1940.

Below: Teenage members of the Danish underground, carrying Sten guns supplied by the British.

Denmark

THE GERMAN ATTACK on Denmark took place at the same time as the attack on Norway. Denmark is a small country, adjacent to Germany, and without any natural barrier to divide it from its southern neighbour: there was therefore no real chance of preventing a German occupation once this became the German plan, nor was there much chance of conducting guerrilla war in a country without forest or mountain. When the Second World War began in 1939, the Danes merely emphasized their traditional policy of strict neutrality, and hoped the Germans would respect it. They also, uniquely, reduced their armed forces *after* the war had broken out.

The Germans expected no trouble, but the general who was to lead the attack took the trouble to visit the country a few days beforehand, in the guise of an ordinary businessman, to have a look round. He observed the lack of defences with satisfaction, and although he did not go so far as to mark down billets for his troops, he might have done so.

The invasion began in the early hours of 9 April 1940. As tanks swept through Jutland, the Luftwaffe flew over Copenhagen in strength. No bombs were dropped, only propaganda leaflets; but within three hours of the attack, the elderly King Christian agreed to surrender. Total casualties on both sides during the invasion of Denmark were about thirty.

For many Danes, the German occupation brought little immediate obvious change. The Germans announced that they did not intend to interfere with the territorial integrity of Denmark, nor with its political independence, and although the latter claim could hardly be maintained, the Germans interfered very little. Business as usual was the order of the day, and the Danes prospered by selling their agricultural produce to the German armies. All Danish institutions remained in being, even the army and navy; there was no harassment of Jews, and no favour was shown to the local fascist party. Nevertheless, freedom had gone. There was, of course, censorship of books and of the press, though at first it was not tremendously strict: banned books could be obtained from Sweden and newspaper readers became adept at reading between the lines. The first underground newspaper did not appear until 1941. Other signs of conquest were the appointment of an allegedly pro-German foreign minister, Erik

Scavenius, and, after June 1941, the arrest of local Communists. When Berlin insisted that Denmark join the Anti-Comintern pact, however, there were demonstrations at Copenhagen university and elsewhere. The anti-German feelings of a large majority of Danes became increasingly obvious and found expression in the policy of the 'cold shoulder', which was also practised by the Dutch. King Christian, though over seventy, continued his daily rides on horseback through the streets of Copenhagen, and managed not to see the salutes of passing Germans while punctiliously acknowledging the greetings of his own subjects. (There are many stories of the King's dignified defiance of the Germans through five years of occupation, but most of them should probably be classed as legends.)

From the first day of the occupation there were acts of sabotage, usually spontaneous acts by angry and frustrated individuals and hardly constituting anything more than a mild nuisance. Meetings of patriotic and anti-German people took place in the various regions, and journalists were active in anti-German propaganda. Because the country was functioning more or less normally and because neutral Sweden was so close, propaganda and intelligence activities were carried out more easily in Denmark than in other occupied countries. Ebbe Munck, foreign correspondent of a Danish newspaper in Sweden but mainly concerned with his job as linkman in an intelligence network, was in touch with SOE before the end of 1940, though nothing came of the contact immediately. The first British-trained agents were dropped into Denmark in September 1941 (one of them had reached England in a small airplane which he had constructed virtually from scratch). SOE had some initial bad luck in Denmark. Of their first pair of parachuted Danes the leader was killed when his parachute failed to open and, as he carried the radio and the names of safe contacts, the second man was left helpless. However, he managed to get in touch with the 'Princes', Danish army officers engaged in supplying intelligence to the British. They were Ebbe Munck's chief suppliers of intelligence (Munck passed on their information to London, where it was very warmly welcomed). Danish intelligence remained excellent throughout the war, and earned high praise from General Eisenhower.

Other resistance activity was less vigorous. The army officers, like the Norwegian military, were trying to build up an underground army which would emerge into the open at the end of the war. In the meantime, they wanted no trouble, and objected even to anti-German propaganda, much to the annoyance of the many Danish exiles, especially young men, who longed to take an active part against the Germans. The British were in an awkward position because, officially, a neutral Danish state still existed, and its government could not be disregarded. There was therefore a tendency to support the passive stance of the Danish army leaders.

By 1942 the most effective sabotage was being carried out by a group whose original members were Communists, though it had picked up so many recruits from the middle class that it was mockingly called the *Borgerlige Partisaner*, Bourgeois Partisans, or BOPA for short. The activities of BOPA and other groups, plus various less violent manifestations of hatred for the Germans, combined with growing paranoia in Berlin, led Hitler to decide on a tougher policy towards Denmark. Seizing on a rather curt reply to a telegram of birthday congratulations he had sent to King Christian, Hitler appointed a 'plenipotentiary', Werner Best, for Denmark, and insisted on a more amenable government, with Scavenius as prime minister. However, Best himself preferred a policy of moderation, and there was little overt change. Denmark was still a 'special case'. In March 1943, a general election was held, the only time such a manifestation of democracy was allowed under Nazi rule. The fascist party received about two per cent of the votes.

Best hoped for a quiet life, and sent rosy reports of Danish peace and security to Berlin, but underneath the surface things were not so peaceful. Sabotage was increasing, and opposition to it from military leaders and others was less firm since an RAF raid had demonstrated what the alternative was: heavy aerial bombing with, inevitably, high civilian casualties. Besides BOPA, numerous smaller groups, such as Holger Danske, which at its largest included about 400 operative personnel, was especially active. These civilian groups received support from SOE, which was sending in agents in greater numbers, including the elegant, colourful and controversial Flemming Muus (who told his story, or part of it, in *The Spark and the Flame*, London 1956). The BBC was pumping out propaganda, and encouraging people to scrawl the 'V' sign on every blank wall, and, most important of all in encouraging resistance, the tide of war could be seen to be turning against the Germans. Strikes, often organized by Communists, were increasing and altogether the government appeared to be losing its grip on the country. In Berlin it was evident that Best's policy of moderation had failed. It was time to get tough. In August Best was summoned to Berlin and reprimanded. An ultimatum was presented to the Danish government which even the pliant Scavenius decided could not be accepted, and the event which had been postponed for nearly two and a half years finally took place. The government resigned, administration was taken over by the permanent heads of the ministries, and the armed forces demobilized. There was little opposition from the Danish soldiers, though one or two units managed to escape as the Danish army was disbanded. The Danish navy, somewhat better prepared, managed to scuttle most of its ships which would otherwise have fallen into German hands.

The German takeover did not immobilize the resistance. Agents, weapons and explosives kept coming, and sabotage continued. A direct effect of the takeover was the creation of the Freedom Council, a seven-man body which included Flemming Muus as senior SOE man in Denmark, to co-ordinate resistance activities (and eventually, at the end of the war,

Top: Members of the underground confront a member of the Danish Royal Ballet suspected of being a member of the SS.

Above: King Christian of Denmark, the focus of Danish patriotic feelings, on one of his regular rides through Copenhagen.

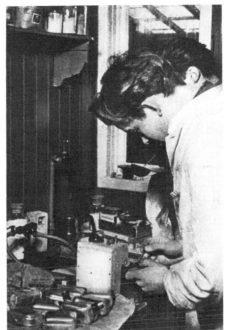

*Top left: Effectively forged papers were
essential to the freedom of movement of
resistance workers in such open societies
as in Denmark.*

*Top right: Simple grenades were made
by saboteurs from everyday materials
such as tins and bottles.*

*Above: A radio receiver was smuggled
in to the concentration camp of Froslev,
where resistance workers were taken.*

Above: Demonstrations in Copenhagen in June and July 1944 were little short of an open revolt against German occupation.

Below: Sabotaging trains, especially those carrying goods to Germany, was perhaps the most important activity of the Danish resistance.

to be incorporated into the liberation government).

A great advantage for the Danes under German rule was the nearness of neutral, but increasingly amiable, Sweden. About 11,000 Danes escaped to Sweden during the course of the war, one or two of them even making it on their own feet, since in the winter it is sometimes possible to walk from Denmark to Sweden over the frozen Baltic. It was the proximity of Sweden which permitted one of the most remarkable successes of the Danish resistance, the rescue of the Jews.

As long as the Germans hoped to make the Danes – impeccable 'Aryans' – their allies and supporters, they refrained from serious persecution of Danish Jews for fear of antagonizing the rest of the population. The crack-down of August 1943 changed the situation and as part of the new tough policy the Germans decided to round up the country's 7,000-odd Jews for deportation. The operation was fixed for the Jewish New Year at the beginning of October, but it was leaked to the resistance by a sympathetic German official, and although some Jews had only a few hours' notice, while others had none at all or ignored the warnings they did get, the majority contrived to be away from home on the night the German soldiers came to arrest them. There followed what Richard Petrow calls 'the greatest mass rescue operation of World War II' (*The Bitter Years*, New York 1974) The vast majority of the Danish Jews escaped to Sweden, which with some courage had announced that, contrary to customary Swedish policy on immigration, it would acept Danish Jews without restriction. Most of the refugees travelled on Danish fishing boats (in some cases paying an extortionate fee), and the Holger Danske group alone operated up to twelve fishing boats during October 1943 which altogether transported about 1,000 Jews. The grand German round-up corralled only about 300 people, including the inhabitants of an old people's home; but, of course, and without detracting from the splendid and courageous behaviour of a great many Danes, the rescue operation could not have been so successful had not a great many Germans been willing to connive at what was going on under their noses. Ordinary German soldiers, however well-trained and obedient to orders, felt at least some distaste at the job they were asked to do, whether or not they were aware of what the ultimate fate of the Jews they were ordered to arrest would be. There were even cases reported of German soldiers knocking on the door of a Jewish family so gently that they failed to wake the people within and quietly went away again when their knock was not answered.

When the Danish armed forces were disbanded in August 1943, the army intelligence officers managed, by and large, to go underground without difficulty. The army command was still, with some exceptions, opposed to sabotage, and there was some friction between the army and civilian resistance groups, as well as between individual civilian groups themselves. One source of friction was the way in which arms smuggled in from Sweden (in remarkably large numbers) often ended up with the army, although the army showed no sign of using them against the Germans. Resistance groups, especially left-wing ones like BOPA, depended on SOE drops and secret workshops for their supplies.

Drops, however, were becoming relatively frequent. Sabotage reached a peak in June 1944, to coincide with the Allied invasion of Normandy. Railway sabotage flourished and BOPA destroyed the Globus factory, which made weapons for the Germans, in a direct attack, suffering only one casualty. These and similar raids brought reprisals. A nasty organization called the Schalburg Corps was let loose to commit retaliatory sabotage against such cherished Danish institutions as the Tivoli Gardens and the Royal Danish Yacht Club. The Germans declared a state of emergency, which only served to provoke strikes and, despite a ban on public gatherings of all kinds, rowdy protest meetings. In several incidents, Germans fired on the crowds and a dozen or more people were killed, with the result that the protest meetings degenerated into riots, with vehicles being overturned and set on fire, barricades being put up in the streets, and more casualties. Plenipotentiary Best, a somewhat debased figure since the military takeover, ordered all public services (fire-fighting, electricity, etc.) in Copenhagen to be cut off.

The country, or sections of it, was only a step away from open revolt. It had all happened spontaneously. The Freedom Council was taken by surprise and unable to make up its collective mind on what action to take. It did, however, give support to the strikers and protesters. Eventually, and no doubt fortunately, a compromise agreement was reached which brought peace (and electricity) back to Copenhagen. Among other concessions, Best agreed to withdraw the Schalburg Corps.

The riots had shown the Germans that the Danish police could not be relied on to enforce German orders upon their countrymen, and in September 1944 the police were suddenly disbanded. Many of them were deported to concentration camps in Germany. To sabotage, which continued on a wide front, was now added a crime wave, not directed primarily against the Germans but really a symptom of frustration and disillusion in society generally. The social atmosphere in Denmark during this last year of the war was tense and unpleasant. To make things worse, the Gestapo was having considerable success against the resistance. In Jutland there were so many arrests that the whole resistance movement seemed to be in danger of annihilation. Desperate measures were called for, and the chief of resistance in Jutland asked, via SOE, for assistance from the Royal Air Force. He asked for the destruction of Gestapo records, which were stored in two houses belonging to the university at Aarhus. The RAF had developed precision bombing to a fairly fine art with its Mosquitoes, light two-man bombers flying fast and low, which carried no guns but relied on speed and manoeuvrability to keep them out of trouble.

The raid took place on the morning of 31 October 1944. Three squadrons of Mosquitoes zoomed in, dropped their bombs, and were gone again before the defences could be mobilized against them. Although several innocent Danes were killed, the Gestapo offices were almost completely destroyed together with a very large number of Gestapo officials: by chance, a big meeting was being held in the building at the time of the raid, attended by Gestapo men from other parts of Jutland.

The success of the Aarhus raid led to plans for a similar attack on Gestapo headquarters in Copenhagen. Here the task was harder and the results less satisfactory. The Gestapo offices were in a largish modern building called the Shellhus, not so easy to identify as the Aarhus university buildings. Moreover, the anti-aircraft defences in Copenhagen were a great deal more effective. Worst of all, the Gestapo kept their prisoners, who included two members of the Freedom Council, in cells on the top two floors, a fact of which they made no secret as their purpose was to discourage attacks of the Aarhus type (the RAF had also raided Gestapo offices successfully in other occupied countries). There was some talk of the Mosquitoes dropping their bombs against the base of the building, but the plain fact was that it was impossible to bomb the Shellhus building without casualties among the Danish prisoners. In the event the raid was carried out on 21 March 1945 with superficial success. The Shellhus was set on fire and Gestapo records destroyed; most of the prisoners, including the Freedom Council men, were unhurt and escaped in the ensuing confusion. However, very few important Gestapo officials were killed because they happened to be out of the building at the time attending the funeral of one of their number who had died of natural causes.

A worse result stemmed from the unfortunate accident that the fourth aeroplane (out of eighteen) to approach the target lost its bearings and crashed into a building near to the Shellhus, exploding on impact and setting the building on fire. As a result, some of the following pilots, misled by the rising column of smoke from the crash, attacked the wrong building. It happened to be a school. Eighty-six Danish children were killed by the RAF's bombs.

When the armistice came, the Germans surrendered without fuss, most of them being only too glad to do so. There was perhaps no great need for the elaborate plans made by the military underground to take over at the end of the war, though they probably prevented some violence and lynchings, as the British reached Denmark well ahead of the Russians. The Red Army had at one time seemed likely to get there first, with possibly dire results for the future of the monarchy and democratic government (the Russians did arrive in the island of Bornholm, and occupied it for the best part of a year before handing it over to the Danish authorities). During the war, the Germans kept about 150,000 troops in Denmark, but unlike the troops stationed in Norway, they were not for the most part front-line troops, and it cannot be said that occupying Denmark was much of a strain on the German war effort.

*One of the many bridges in S Norway
destroyed by the Norwegians to slow the
German military advance in the spring
of 1940.*

Norway

DURING THE GREAT WAR of 1914-18 Norway, like Sweden and Denmark, had remained neutral. The Norwegians had every intention of following the same course in the 1930s, but they were disappointed. The *Altmark* incident showed how difficult it could be to stay uninvolved.

The *Altmark* was a German supply vessel carrying a large number of British prisoners of war who had been released from the *Graf Spee* before that famous battleship had been scuttled off the River Plate. Early in 1940 the *Altmark* entered Norwegian waters on her way home to Germany. The British asserted that by transporting prisoners of war through neutral waters she was infringing the rules of neutrality, and the Norwegians stopped her. Her captain claimed that, as a warship she was not liable to inspection and the Norwegians, wanting to avoid what promised to become a very awkward situation indeed, managed to search the ship without finding the prisoners. The British thereupon sent a force into Norwegian waters to capture the *Altmark* and release the prisoners, an action which gave the British people something to savour and put Hitler in a rage.

Norway's strategic position was just too important. Her indented coastline offered numerous sheltered bases which the Germans might use to launch raids on North Atlantic shipping. The Arctic port of Narvik was an important outlet, during the winter months, for iron ore from northern Sweden, a vital commodity for the German war effort. These considerations were well known in Britain and in Germany, and from the earliest days of the war there was pressure from various elements in both London and Berlin to make sure of Norway. When action came, the Germans were ahead—as the British force which had been assembled for duty in Norway during the Finno-Russian war of 1940 had been sent to France instead when the peace talks began in March.

Hitler stated his intention of invading Norway (and Denmark) on 1 March 1940. The German general staff did not expect much resistance from the natives, but the manner of the attack—by sea, and aimed at chief ports such as Narvik and Trondheim—was very daring, as Britain still commanded the sea. In the event, the Germans had a good deal of luck and the British were at certain points a little too slow-witted, otherwise the Scandinavian assault might conceivably have ended in a disaster which would have brought Hitler down.

On 7 April, when the ships were at sea, the weather turned nasty, with gales and poor visibility. Destroyer escorts were broken up and assault troops arrived at their destinations feeling very much the worse for seasickness; but the bad visibility favoured the Germans. Narvik was the scene of stern resistance, but at Trondheim the German ships tied up at the city quays as if they were on a good-will visit, and there were no troops to prevent the soldiers taking over. At Bergen the defenders were more alert and the city had been blacked out, but unfortunately this measure also blacked out the searchlights that were supposed to light up attacking ships for the port guns. One German cruiser was damaged, but again the troops to defend the city itself were not present. Oslo gave more trouble. The heavy cruiser *Blücher* was sunk in the Narrows as the naval force approached, and the other ships withdrew, but Oslo subsequently fell to airborne troops.

Thereafter, the Germans met stiff resistance in some places, especially when they approached the mountains, where their vastly superior mobility was less of an advantage. The government withdrew ahead of them and King Haakon got away to England on a British destroyer on 7 June, after calling for continued resistance to the Germans.

The British, having failed more or less dismally to intercept the German invasion forces at sea, hastened to retrieve the position, if they could. British and French troops mounted an attack on Trondheim but, to the disgust of the Norwegian commander, they were inferior in numbers, ill-equipped and without air support. They were soon ordered to withdraw. 'So Norway is to go the way of Poland and Czechoslovakia,' the Norwegian commander commented bitterly.

The British were more successful at Narvik, where the entire German naval strength at the port was blasted by the battleship *Warspite*, last in action in 1916; but having recaptured the town with Polish help on 28 May, the troops were soon withdrawn again to help in the defence of Britain.

The national socialist leader Vidkun Quisling seized the opportunity to declare himself prime minister. He was soon removed by the Germans, though he returned 18 months later. The real governor of the country, however, was Reichskommissar Joseph Terboven, a squalid old-time Nazi, whose first act was to shackle the press and launch a major propaganda campaign denigrating the exiled king (who refused to abdicate) and praising National Socialism. A tame ministry was installed, including members of Quisling's party, and a campaign started to bring, in particular, the professional classes to heel. First on the list was the law: all the judges of the Supreme Court resigned on being informed that they should obey the decree of the Reichskommissar. Next came the Lutheran Church: the bishops protested against the regime's violence and the political dismissal of pastors. There were mass resignations from all professional organizations as fascists were put into official positions, but shadow organizations continued to exist unofficially.

When Quisling became head of the government in February 1942, he directed his attention particularly to the schools, where future generations of Norwegians could be indoctrinated at the most appropriate age. The teaching profession was to be nazified like the others, and all members of it were advised to join the Teachers' Organization The result was, for Quisling, disappointing. Out of 14,000 teachers, all but 2,000 rejected the Teachers' Organization and despatched letters of protest. This was civilian resistance on a massive scale. Many hundreds of teachers were arrested and sent to Jørstadmoen concentration camp near Lillehammer. Some 700 were sent to perform forced labour in the Arctic on a filthy, overcrowded and insanitary ship which shocked even the fascist medical officer, whose protest was ignored by Quisling. Under this savage treatment, a few teachers naturally gave in, but the great majority still refused to join the Teachers' Organization and in the end it was Quisling who had to surrender. In May the schools reopened after two months' closure, and little more was heard of the Teachers' Organization.

Quisling also stepped up the persecution of the Jews. Four were executed without trial on a charge of spreading news learned from a BBC broadcast. Property was confiscated, and there were arbitrary arrests. All Jews had to report their whereabouts to the police; there was a form for doing this which was even given to Jews who were already in police custody. Some 700 Norwegian Jews reached Sweden but 760 were transported to Germany. Only 24 returned.

However, the German occupying forces on the whole behaved very well in Norway. As long as he steered clear of the Gestapo the ordinary Norwegian citizen might find them reasonably agreeable. The different behaviour of the Germans in different countries was an important factor in resistance activity: the Norwegians were a Nordic race and therefore quite acceptable to the German racist doctrine. They were not treated like, for example, the Poles. Public opinion, despite the underground press, was strongly against provoking the Germans. Resistance activity was slow to develop, and at first amounted to little more than a few groups of students and young people forming sports clubs and doing exercises which might be regarded as vaguely military; they had no weapons. Army officers also formed underground groups taking orders from the army leaders. Yet Quisling's fascist party increased its numbers from 4,000 to 23,750 between January and December 1940.

Gradually, the little ex-army groups linked up to form an organization known as Milorg (Military Organization). Its aims were modest and long-term. It was mainly concerned with planning for an Allied invasion and with what would happen when the Germans were defeated. Milorg's leaders were, at first, politically conservative army officers (but tactics did not change much when it was led by a lawyer in his twenties). They were concerned to build up, slowly, a national organization which would take control when the Germans left (Milorg was, in November, recognized by the Norwegian government in exile, though at first it kept its distance). Milorg was not even especially interested in getting arms from Britain. Security was bad, as it usually is in underground movements in an open society or those run by professional military men.

There were also, of course, many younger, more aggressive Norwegians prepared to risk anything to get into the fight against the Germans. A surprising number got to Britain where they might be vetted and, if suitable, employed by SOE, who sent their first agent to Norway in December 1940. Among them was Martin Linge, a well-known actor who became a charismatic leader of commando forces during his brief career. Such men were more in tune with the aims of SOE, which were to make every German-occupied country as troublesome as possible to the occupying forces.

Linge took part, as leader of his Norwegian company, in the first Lofotens raid in March 1941, which was followed by arrests and reprisals against those who had helped the invaders, or who had relatives who had gone away with the British. The Norwegian government in London protested that it had not been consulted and Milorg deplored all raids and acts of sabotage in a long letter of complaint. Despite efforts to improve them, relations between SOE and Milorg continued rather frosty, and they were exacerbated by the second Lofotens raid of Christmas week 1941. The population of the Lofotens were not unnaturally furious when the British again withdrew after seizing the islands, leaving them to the mercies of the Germans.

Reprisals also followed the discovery of SOE agents in Norway, several of whom were given away by an insidious Nazi sympathizer in the underground movement. Except for the famous 'Shetland Bus', SOE's maritime link with Norway run by Norwegian fishermen which smuggled many people in or out of the country, the Norwegian resistance was in generally poor shape in 1942. One arrest led to another, and the snowballing process gave the Germans the opportunity to annihilate the whole resistance movement. Milorg was wiped out in most parts of the country, and virtually every SOE agent was rounded up or shot resisting arrest.

In view of its limited role, the Norwegian resistance might seem to have been of little use in the war effort up to 1943, but that is not altogether true. At the very least, it was a useful cover for raids, campaigns and projects against the Germans in other parts of Europe, and kept many fighting men busy. It was not entirely, or even primarily, the ineptitude of the Norwegians that was the cause of the near total destruction of the military resistance organization, but rather the powerful effort and determination of the Germans to destroy possible sources of revolt in Norway. Hitler always believed that the British would launch a major campaign in Norway (and indeed, if Churchill had had his way, Hitler's guess would have been right), and it was therefore particularly important to prevent a rising within the country to coincide, perhaps, with an Allied invasion. It was partly for this reason too that so many big ships like the *Tirpitz* were stationed in Norwegian waters when, arguably, they might have been better employed in another theatre.

The most famous exploit of Norwegians against the Germans in the Second World War was the raid on the Norsk Hydro factory at Vemork, Telemarken, south Norway. The incident (described by a participant, Knut Haukelid, in his book *Skis Against the Atom*, London 1954) is justly famous because it was well-planned, perfectly executed and unique.

The significance of Norsk Hydro was that it was the only European manufacturer of heavy water on any worthwhile scale. In heavy water (D_2O), the two atoms of hydrogen in a molecule of ordinary water (H_2O) are replaced by two atoms of deuterium, or heavy hydrogen. Heavy water has different characteristics from ordinary water. Its boiling point and freezing point are higher, its density is greater, and its molecular weight is 20, compared to 18 for ordinary water, hence its name. German scientists wanted heavy water in experiments to produce atomic energy; they needed it as a moderating agent to slow down fast neutrons so that they would fission uranium-235 and begin a chain reaction. We now know that German atomic physics was less advanced than was supposed, but at the time it was a reasonable assumption that if Germany could be deprived of heavy water, it would be prevented from making an atomic bomb.

Some months before the invasion of Norway, representatives of a German chemical combine called on Norsk Hydro to ask if they could supply 100 kg of heavy water a month for an indefinite time. The Germans would also buy the stock on hand. The Norwegians were surprised: heavy water was produced merely as a by-product of electrolysis at the Vemork works, in a quantity about one-tenth of the amount required by the Germans, who would not say what they wanted the stuff for. Soon afterwards, Norsk Hydro were approached by the French with a similar request. But the French were more forthcoming and told the Norwegians why they, and thus by inference the Germans, wanted large quantities of heavy water. The Norwegians hastily sold what was available to France, while informing the Germans that they were unable to fulfil their requirements.

Six months later the Germans were in possession of Norway and no longer had to ask the Norwegians for anything. Although they had lost what heavy water was in stock, they were in a position to appropriate all future production, and to raise the monthly output to the rate they wanted.

British intelligence did not become aware of the significance of the Vemork works and its heavy-water production immediately, but by the end

Above: A Norwegian band illegally marching under the windows of an Oslo hospital to raise the morale of resistance workers taken there from prison camps.

Opposite: A fishing boat on the 'Shetland Bus' route, established in 1940 as the main supply route for men and materials for the Norwegian resistance workers.

Left: A member of Milorg on patrol.

Below: Vidkun Quisling encouraged the German invasion in his desire to create a 'Greater Norway'.

of 1941 its importance as a target for destruction was generally agreed. A Norwegian scientist who had been engaged in setting up the factory sent reports of vastly increased production, and in March 1942 the British dropped an agent into Norway who established contacts in the Vemork plant. His name was Einar Skinnarland, and he had been in England only twelve days (he had arrived in the steamer *Galtesund*, which was captured by a group of young men in order to make their escape to England). Skinnarland's absence from his native country was never noticed, and he was soon sending reports which put the motives for increased heavy-water production at Vemork beyond doubt. The destruction of the plant was discussed in the cabinet as a matter of high priority.

The position of the factory made bombing extremely difficult. It was a long way away, almost at the limit of a bomber's range in 1942. It was built on the side of a steep slope above a narrow valley, in wooded, mountainous country often under cloud cover. If bombers managed to hit the factory at all, they might not hit the vital part, nor destroy the tanks of existing stock. The job was therefore given to the Commandos. Two Halifaxes towed gliders full of troops which were to land on the Hardanger Plateau. A four-man party of SOE-trained Norwegians was dropped to prepare the way (they were dropped 150 km off-target, and had a gruelling ski trip in sub-zero temperatures before they reached the rendezvous). In early November, the Commandos followed them.

This airborne operation was a total disaster. The first Halifax crashed into mountains near the Norwegian coast, the second could not find the lighted landing area and also crashed, but its tow rope broke and its glider landed in the sea. There were a few survivors from both gliders; all of them were captured and shot by the Germans in accordance with Hitler's order of execution for all Commandos. The four-man SOE party, left without means of returning, lasted the winter in a remote mountaineers' hut, living on reindeer meat.

The Norsk Hydro plant now became the object of a 'special operation'. SOE could call upon several Norwegians who, besides the uncommon qualities required for sophisticated sabotage in a mountainous, wintry and well-guarded country, also knew the Norsk Hydro factory from personal experience or through studying a detailed model made for the purpose in England. The party consisted of six men under Lieutenant Joachim Ronneberg who, having left their final messages to their families with SOE to be delivered if, as seemed more than likely, they did not survive, took off from Wick, in the north of Scotland, in January. On the first attempt, the pilot could not find the landing lights lit by the original four who had performed the same operation for the Commandos, but at the next full moon the team dropped safely on to Lake Skryken, which was of course frozen. As a welcome, the weather immediately blew up into a ferocious blizzard which kept them confined to a fortuitous woodman's shelter for nearly a week. On 23 February the two groups at last made contact, and on the following day, Ronneberg and his group set out on skis for Vemork. They found shelter a mile or two from the narrow valley on the opposite side of which lay their objective, and considered ways of reaching it. There was a suspension bridge across the valley, but it was guarded and there was no way of silencing the sentries without an alarm being raised. The alternative was to descend to the bottom of the valley and climb up, through trees and rocks, on the other side. The drawback to this method was that such a climb was reputed to be impossible, and for men carrying arms and explosives, in the dark, it seemed out of the question. However, careful examination through binoculars revealed a possible way up.

On the night of 27 February, Ronneberg and his men, having stashed their skis in a safe place, were crouching among the trees opposite the Norsk Hydro works, glowing and glimmering on the other side of the ravine. They descended to the valley bottom, crossing the fast-flowing but partly frozen river, and, searching for handholds in the snow, climbed the cliff-like slope beyond in surprisingly fast time. Well before midnight they were laid up only two or three hundred metres from the main buildings. Taking advantage of sentry-changing, they cut the wire fence and gained the inside of the factory compound. There they split up into three teams—two demolition teams and one covering force, stationed a few metres away from the building where the German guards were sleeping. There was no need to be particularly careful about noise because the noise of the generators blanketed the sound of footsteps or conversation.

One of the demolition teams had to break a window to get into the part of the factory where the electrolytic cells were located, but otherwise all went smoothly. There was only a sleepy Norwegian watchman inside, and the charges were soon laid. Two minutes later (fuses had to be short to make sure of success) the tanks of heavy water were demolished in a muted explosion: the operation was so precise that only a minimum charge was needed and several minutes passed before German guards appeared to investigate. The Norwegians were already on the far side of the valley, making their way back along the route they had come, before the alarm was raised at the factory. Eighteen days later Ronneberg and his party appeared in Sweden, after a journey of over 500 km. The others went into hiding in Norway.

Although the sabotage at Vemork was a brilliantly successful operation from any point of view, the Germans managed to repair the damage in a remarkably short time. British intelligence had estimated that the raid would put heavy-water production back by two years, but in fact the factory was in operation in less than four months. In November it was bombed by an American force of about 150 B17s. The total weight of bombs dropped by the Americans was approximately 10,000 times the weight of the explosives used by the Norwegian saboteurs eight months previously. The power station was destroyed and production stopped until the end of the war. But the stocks of heavy water were not destroyed.

One result of the visit of the American bombers was that the Germans decided to move the existing stocks of heavy water – some 12,000 kg – from Vemork to Germany, together with some equipment. Thanks to Skinnarland, still with contacts at the plant, British intelligence soon learned of this decision. In January, Skinnarland informed London of the date of the move, which was only a few days ahead, and Lt Haukelid, who had taken part in the raid on the plant, was assigned the task of discovering the proposed route and taking action to stop the goods reaching their destination. He reported that the best chance was to attack the ferry which would transport the tanks across Lake Tinnsjö, between rail terminals. Although it was bound to mean the loss of Norwegian lives, Haukelid prepared to sabotage the ferry. With one companion, he gained access to the ferry the night before it was due to sail. They were discovered by a Norwegian guard, but he proved patriotic and kept his mouth shut when they told him they were escaping from the Gestapo. They placed explosive in the bows of the ship so that the explosion would lift her stern and give her no chance of reaching shore, and the charges were timed to go off when the ferry was over the deepest part of the lake – a nice calculation, since Haukelid had to take into account such factors as the customary late starting of this particular ferryboat. Having set the charges, Haukelid slipped off the boat and began his own belated journey to Sweden, which he reached safely two days later.

The explosion occurred on schedule at 10.45 am, when the ferry was in 400 metres of water. Water pouring in at the bows sent the stern up, and wagons containing the heavy-water tanks rolled forward and off the boat, preceding her to the bottom. Twenty-six people were drowned, but the heavy water had gone for good.

The American raid on the Norsk Hydro works was not the only massive bomber onslaught against Norwegian targets. An American raid took place in July 1943 against an industrial complex near Oslo, with heavy civilian casualties. The Norwegian government in exile was not informed of either raid in advance, and protested strongly when it heard the results. The Allies' tactics also had some effect in confirming Milorg in their argument in favour of sabotage. The government in London still favoured passive resistance, but Milorg's younger men were becoming more vociferous in support of an active policy. The civilian resistance was against any military planning on a large scale that might provoke the Germans, including the making of plans for action in the event of an Allied invasion of Norway. The Communists, a small but militant group who criticized the caution of Milorg, were active proponents of sabotage.

By 1943 the underground generally was much better organized, and security was much tighter, though the cost of this improvement was a great deal of administrative work which, in the minds of younger people at any rate, was but dimly connected with resistance against the Germans.

Some military supplies were dropped in 1943-44, certainly more than in the previous two years, yet Milorg remained largely an army without arms. Pressed by the British, often with the support of the government in exile, Milorg carried out a number of sabotage operations against factories and fuel dumps. A group that became known as the Oslo Gang caused more or less serious disruption in various industries in the Oslo area. In factories where Communist influence was strong, the workers themselves some-times organized sabotage, though they had little in the way of explosives and were not often able to get supplies from a disapproving Milorg.

There were some who wished to stage a national uprising in the wake of the Allied invasion of Normandy, but this had been expressly forbidden in London, and Eisenhower's headquarters advised Milorg directly that no operation was planned in Scandinavia and therefore no help could be given to an anti-German rising in Norway. Much heroic blood might have been preserved if such a message had been sent to other underground armies in occupied Europe at a similarly vital moment.

Thus Milorg retained its primarily protective role until the end, or almost the end. As Germany's inevitable defeat was seen to be drawing near, Milorg leaders pressed for a more active role. The achievements of the French Resistance in helping the Allied forces after D-Day led the Allied headquarters to encourage resistance in other countries to a greater extent than before; Milorg was asked to launch a full-scale attack on transportation, in particular, to prevent German troops in Norway reinforcing von Rundstedt in the Ardennes.

In the winter months of 1944-45 Norwegian troops had supported the advance into Finnmark, in the extreme north-east corner of Norway, of the Soviet armies of liberation. As the Germans retreated they removed or destroyed everything that could be of any possible use to their enemies, even deporting the population. Though the Russian tanks were surpris-ingly mobile, considering they were operating inside the Arctic Circle, the cold weather and the 'scorched-earth' policy slowed the advance. The Norwegians had one or two small clashes with the Germans–they were forced to drive them out of Alta airport, for example–but the Germans were never defeated in Norway. Their army, still some 350,000 strong, surrendered only because of the surrender on the European continent. ('Clench your teeth, keep discipline, obey orders,' said their commander.) The Russians, to the considerable relief of the government, immediately withdrew from Norwegian territory, and on 7 May Milorg, which had been greatly strengthened in the previous months by SOE men dropped in to prepare for the German withdrawal, finally emerged from underground to take over industrial plants, defences and other strategic points, to accept the German surrender, and to ensure a smooth transfer of authority. Allied regular troops began arriving two days later, and on 7 June, King Haakon returned to his country five years to the day after he had left it, and by the same kind of transport–a British destroyer.

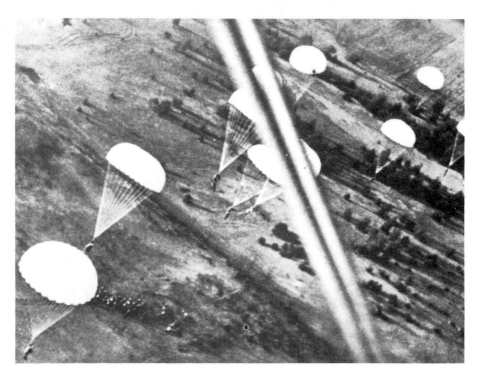

Above: German parachutists landing in Holland during the invasion of May 1940.

Below: Resistance workers planting explosives by a roadside to ambush a German convoy.

Netherlands

BRITISH INTELLIGENCE and irregular warfare organizations were singularly unfortunate (or incompetent) in the Netherlands, and this is paradoxical for the Netherlands in some ways might have offered particularly fruitful ground for their enterprises. No nation was more solidly anti-German, and no nation has found it harder to forgive and forget.

An ominous portent of British failure in the Netherlands was an incident at Venlo in November 1939.

British intelligence had for a long time maintained an operational base in Holland. The Dutch, in general sympathetic towards the British, had known of its existence for almost as long. It was one of those secret operations, all too common in the shadowy world of intelligence, which are hidden from everybody except those people who are really not meant to know. For example, until a few years ago, the identity of the chief of the British secret service was never uttered except in code and as a result the ordinary Britisher in the street did not know who he was. But the Russians, of course, knew perfectly well. Allen Dulles was more sensible when, years later, he decided to make no bones about it and mark the headquarters of the CIA in Washington with a brass plate on the door. He found he was less troubled with gawping tourists thereafter.

The trouble with MI6's organization in The Hague was not that Dutch intelligence knew all about it: that was probably necessary. More significantly, the Germans knew about it too. Every one who called at Captain Payne Best's canalside office was carefully photographed by the Germans from the other side of the canal.

Soon after the outbreak of the war in September, Payne Best established contact with, as he thought, a senior German officer sympathetic to the British. A meeting was arranged for Venlo, a town on the Dutch-German frontier, and Payne Best travelled in company with another MI6 man, from London, and a Dutch officer, sent along at the insistence of General van Oorschot, chief of Dutch military intelligence (though not for much longer; Venlo was the end for him too). When they reached the meeting place, a café on the Dutch side of the frontier, they were seized by an SS commando and hustled across the border. The leader of this German operation incidentally was the officer who had organized the fake attack by 'Poles' who were actually German prisoners dressed up in Polish uniforms on a German radio station at Gleiwitz which had been the 'provocation' for Germany's attack on Poland. This new enterprise provided useful evidence for justifying the infringement of Dutch neutrality, which was beginning to appear inevitable.

Incidentally, it would be interesting to know exactly what the British were up to at Venlo. It has been suggested that the secret service was being used by the prime minister, Neville Chamberlain, to investigate the possibilities of a compromise peace with Hitler behind the backs of his Cabinet colleagues.

The Netherlands is a small country, notoriously flat for the most part, with land frontiers almost impossible to defend against a far mightier continental neighbour. In the past, the Dutch had performed miracles of defence by manipulation of their dikes and locks, but in the age of the bomber and the paratrooper, these watery defences were not likely to prove much of an obstacle. The Dutch, with little choice, placed their hopes in neutrality, a policy which had served them successfully during the Great War of 1914-18. For what it was worth, Hitler's government had stated as late as August 1939 that Dutch neutrality would be respected. When the Germans invaded Poland a week or two later, the Dutch reaffirmed their neutrality, although they also mobilized their army. The outbreak of war was a severe economic blow to the Dutch who were heavily dependent on trade, because of the severe inhibitions it placed on shipping. There was also little doubt, though perhaps the Germans were not fully aware of it, on which side Dutch sympathies lay.

The Dutch had reports of a German invasion within a few days of the Venlo incident, but it did not materialize. That this was merely a postponement, not a cancellation, was proved by the activities of German agents, who were found to be passing information regarding Dutch defence works and also smuggling Dutch military uniforms out of the country, which suggested that another Gleiwitz was on the cards. The Dutch government pulled in its belt, arrested a handful of home-grown Nazis, and prepared for the worst.

It did not come for nearly six months. On 9 May, the Dutch military attaché in Berlin signalled home, 'Tomorrow at dawn. Hold tight.' At 3 am on 10 May, German troops crossed the frontier. Dutch airfields were bombed and the Dutch air force knocked out at a blow, while paratroopers descended on strategic targets such as the Moerdijk bridge across the Rhine estuary. One group landed at The Hague in an attempt to capture the Queen and the government, but they were defeated. Prince Bernhard, the German-born husband of Crown Princess Juliana, himself had a few shots at the attackers among the rose bushes in the palace gardens.

Elsewhere the Germans were overwhelmingly successful. The Queen and government departed on two British destroyers for London, which was declared the seat of government. After the bombing of Rotterdam while negotiations for surrender were actually taking place (probably the result of a communications failure rather than mere Nazi brutality), General Winkelman announced that the Dutch had surrendered, after four and a half days of war.

As in other western European countries, the German occupation of the Netherlands was at first relatively mild, but became progressively more harsh.

The Dutch, like it or not (and mostly they do not), are closely related to the Germans. From a Nazi viewpoint, they were Aryans and therefore racially acceptable. There was some hope of gaining the support of the population at large, though in fact the number of German sympathizers was, and remained, small. In February 1941, moves against Dutch Jews by the Germans and the Dutch Nazis provoked a strike in Amsterdam. The strike was short but incurred severe reprisals, and it marked a sharp deterioration, exacerbated by the entry of the Soviet Union and the United States into the war, which encouraged hope–and therefore opposition–in occupied Europe. Further deterioration set in when in 1943 the Germans, under increasing pressure, began to extract every available ounce of war material and manpower from the conquered countries. From the summer of 1943, there were increasing acts of violence including assassination, murder of hostages, and sabotage. A situation close to open war existed between resistance groups on one hand and the Nazi authorities–Dutch and German–on the other.

Topographical conditions alone made partisan warfare as practised in Yugoslavia, for example, an impossibility in the Netherlands. Resistance of one kind or another was nevertheless widespread.

The underground press in the Netherlands was remarkably prolific, and the first mimeographed hand-written news-sheet appeared the day after the surrender. A list of clandestine publications of one kind or another between 1940 and 1945, compiled by the Netherlands Institute for War Documentation, contains nearly 1,200 titles. Some of them were short-lived, and print runs were usually small (though exceeding a total of half a million in 1943), but each copy was passed from hand to hand, so that total readership was certainly large though incalculable.

The groups producing the early papers were occasionally involved in active resistance, including sabotage of a disorganized kind, more satisfying to the perpetrators than damaging to the Germans and usually leading, sooner or later, to the arrest and execution of those involved. Later, more substantial papers were established, which maintained publication for long periods. *Vrij Nederland* (Free Netherlands), a well-printed paper first produced in August 1940, lasted the whole period of occupation, mainly under one editor, H. M. van Randwijk. He was arrested once by the Germans but released. Some 70 others were executed or died in

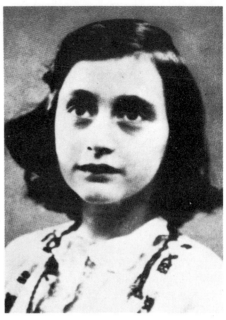

Above: Mrs. Kuipers-Rietberg established the largest organization to help escapees and other people on the run in Holland.

Above: Anne Frank, the Jewish girl whose diary is one of the most moving human records of the Second World War.

Opposite: Franz Goedhart, the best-known anti-Nazi writer in the Netherlands under his pseudonym Pieter 't Hoen.

Top: A satirical poster on the plight of the Dutch press under German occupation.

Above: The Germans opened the dikes and flooded vast areas of the Netherlands in June 1944 to supplement their defences.

concentration camps as a result of working for *Vrij Nederland*. The editor of *Het Parool*, who wrote under the name Pieter 't Hoen (Peter the Chicken) was caught when trying to make a getaway to England. The Germans knew he was connected with *Het Parool*, but did not realize he was the famous Pieter 't Hoen, and as the paper continued to appear with articles bearing his *nom de plume*, to throw the Germans off the scent, they never did identify him. He was sentenced to death nonetheless, but risked revealing his identity to the Dutch policemen, who helped him escape a few days before the day set for his execution. He returned to his underground editorial desk and the Germans never knew he had left it.

There were two or three other major papers besides *Vrij Nederland* and *Het Parool*, reflecting various political and/or religious standpoints, and a whole host of lesser publications, some concerned as much with future Dutch society as with resistance to the Germans, and others reflecting the interests of different sections of the population. There was even a paper published by Indonesian students at Leiden which concentrated on current events in Asia, and there were instances of ordinary legal newspapers being compelled by resistance groups to print one underground edition daily. Many pamphlets and books were also printed by the Dutch underground press, books in English and French as well as Dutch. Especially popular were accounts of how the Dutch had thrown off Spanish rule in the 17th century, a story the moral of which was not hard to draw under German occupation.

Many acts of resistance were carried out in the early days of the occupation by furious and defiant individuals or organizations without much plan or purpose. However, organizations were swiftly formed to oppose the Germans. Many of these, at least in the first year or two, attempted only non-militant forms of opposition. (The Dutch proved to be experts at passive resistance, and the total silence that fell whenever a German entered a crowded room or a bar was not a totally insignificant means of resistance.) But these resistance organizations, like the underground publications with which some were connected, remained separate bodies, as in other countries, representing different doctrines and different notions on how to deal with the current crisis. Though the Dutch like the French spoke of 'the Resistance', it was never a single, unified movement.

The *Orde Dienst* (Order Service), was a small though nationwide organization run mainly by army officers, and it was largely concerned with the preservation of law and order in the interval between German defeat and restoration of the legal government, though it also endeavoured to hasten that time by anti-German espionage and sabotage. The *Orde Dienst* aroused doubt and suspicion because of its rather right-wing stance and its lack of whole-hearted commitment to action against the Germans, though it would seem that these fears were baseless.

A major task of Dutch resistance was to look after the 'divers' (*onderduikers*) or 'bikers' (*fietsers*), i.e. people in hiding from the authorities, and two of the largest organizations were primarily concerned with this. One of them, claiming 15,000 helpers by 1945, was founded by a Calvinist minister and a housewife and mother (Mrs Kuipers-Rietberg, who was arrested in 1944, and died in a concentration camp). It is said to have distributed 220,000 false ration books per month in 1944. The first 'divers' were usually Jews, but later an increasing number were men evading labour in Germany and former soldiers evading internment. The Dutch were perhaps the least anti-Semitic people in Europe; nevertheless, the efforts to save Dutch Jews were not all that successful. There were about 140,000 Jews in the Netherlands in 1940. By 1945, just over 30,000 were still alive—and most of them were in concentration camps. Such figures are grim but lack emotion. A more compelling memorial to the dead is the diary of one Jew in the Netherlands who did not survive: a little girl, Anne Frank.

It was difficult to establish contacts with the British services engaged in encouraging opposition to the Germans in occupied Europe, especially after the fiasco at Venlo. The Germans made a clean sweep of MI6's operatives in the Netherlands thanks to their record of visitors to Payne Best's office and to the list of names found in the pocket of Payne Best's companion at Venlo. The first agent, von Hamel, set up a fine intelligence network August–October 1940, but a young naval officer named Zomer, parachuted in with a radio transmitter in the summer of 1941, was picked up ten weeks later in possession of a number of radio messages in code and in clear, from which the German cryptologist, Ernst May, rapidly deduced the whole cipher system. Zomer was 'turned around' by the Germans, but managed to let London know that he and his transmitter were in enemy hands, so no great harm was done.

A very different matter was Operation North Pole, otherwise known as *Englandspiel*, the worst defeat suffered by SOE throughout the war. The part of SOE concerned with the Netherlands was known as N Section, and it worked in co-operation with a Dutch unit in London commanded by Colonel de Bruijne. From the start affairs in the Netherlands were handled with an astonishing lack of imagination from London. Agents were fixed up with clothes, well tailored, with every clue to their English manufacture carefully expunged. But, except for size, each suit of clothes, right down to socks and tie, was exactly the same. The unfortunate agents might as well have worn uniform.

This would not have mattered if no agents had been caught, but, as a result of terrible lapses in London, and equally of skilful work by Germans like May, Josef Schreider, and the *Abwehr* chief, H. J. Giskes, many were.

In March 1942, a simple security operation in The Hague resulted in the arrest of an SOE radio operator named Lauwers, who had been betrayed by a Dutchman. The Germans also knew, pretty well, current cipher methods, thanks to other arrests and to the work of Ernst May. Lauwers was not particularly troubled when the Germans forced him to continue transmitting to London, the standard tactic with captured radio operators (and used with brilliant success in England), because he assumed London would draw the correct conclusion when he omitted his security check – a personal signal that each operator included in every message to prove he was still a free agent. But to Lauwers' consternation, London did not notice. Or rather, they did notice, but assumed that the check had been left out by mistake.

Things went from bad to worse. London asked Lauwers to prepare a reception for another agent, and when this man arrived, he found his reception committee consisted not of Dutch resistance workers but the Gestapo. It was such a devastating shock that he revealed more information than he might have done. More agents were despatched, landed exactly where the Germans, through their captured transmitters, had instructed, and gave away more information.

The unfortunate Lauwers not only omitted his security check from the messages he transmitted, he even managed, on three occasions, to transmit the letters 'cau... ght' without the Germans noticing. Unfortunately, the British did not notice either, though they did advise another captured agent that he ought to use his security check – thus placing his life in imminent danger. Lauwers endeavoured to contact the British, in other ways. He smuggled a letter out of his cell with a coded warning, but the letter never reached its destination.

Between March 1942 and May 1943, over fifty agents were dropped directly into German hands. Five escaped, and two, by generous help, good luck and brilliance, got to Switzerland and thence, via France and Spain returned to London to spill the beans. Meanwhile, the Germans had not been idle and had passed on the information that the two escapees had gone over to them. When they arrived in London they were sent to prison.

The Germans dealt skilfully with attempts by N Section, getting a bit concerned by its lack of results, to carry out a double check. Several times Giskes despatched supposed agents to make personal contact via one of the escape lines, only for the said agents to be 'arrested' somewhere along the line before contact was made.

Englandspiel came to an end with this broadcast, *en clair*, to London on All Fools' Day, 1 April 1944:

'Messrs. Blunt, Bingham [commanders of N section] and Successors Ltd. London. In the last time you are trying to make business in Netherlands without our assistance. We think this rather unfair in view of our long and successful co-operation as your sole agents. But never mind, whenever you will come to pay a visit to the continent you may be assured that you will be received with the same care and result as all those you sent us before. So long.'

In a brief account, extenuating circumstances tend to be ignored. The full story of North Pole, for which there is not space here, reveals the

British to have been less hopelessly inefficient and irresponsible than a summary of the main events makes them appear. All the same, it was a shocking episode.

Among Dutch resistance organizations, the most vigorous was the *Raad van Verzet* (RVV), founded in the spring of 1943 by Jan Thijssen and other people anxious to take more positive action against the Germans. It was initially independent-minded and hot-headed, but later became more responsible and more amenable to advice from London. Although it took part in espionage and escape activities, the main business was sabotage. One of its first acts, in fact predating its formal foundation, was the raid on the registry of births in Amsterdam, in which records were burned to make it more difficult to ferret out Jews. The RVV was responsible for assassinations of traitors and German agents in the resistance. It was the main recipient of arms supplied from Britain, and the main instigator of acts of sabotage from 1944 onwards.

In the early years, sabotage was limited and never more than a very minor irritant to the Germans. Communications were cut, tyres slashed, petrol tanks punctured, and machinery destroyed. There was a good deal of surreptitious industrial sabotage of the kind that could conceivably be ascribed to accidents. Some weapons were stolen and stored for the anticipated day of revolt, though they were few compared with the drops made by SOE from August 1944. Activity of this kind increased after the Allied armies had landed in France and the railway system was subjected to frequent dislocation. Altogether, though, sabotage in the Netherlands had little military significance, and the attempt of certain resistance groups to link up with the Allied forces at Arnhem were unsuccessful.

When Belgium was liberated in September 1944, the Dutch naturally hoped and expected that their turn would soon follow. But except for the southern provinces, they were doomed to another winter of German occupation, and much the worst winter they had so far suffered. All traces of conciliation in German policy had vanished; the Germans were merely intent on defending their crumbling empire at almost any price, carrying out savage acts of reprisal for opposition. Hardship for ordinary people was increased by resistance activities: the railway strike coinciding with the Arnhem landings continued after the defeat of that enterprise, and in retaliation the Germans placed a ban on the movement of food. Many people survived on a diet of sugar beet and tulip bulbs, and in the western part of the country thousands actually died of hunger.

The so-called Forces of the Interior, under the command of Prince Bernhard, were established in the autumn of 1944, and the main resistance organizations were incorporated with them. When German defeat became inevitable, a committee of underground leaders was appointed to negotiate with the Germans, but in April 1945 the negotiations were taken over by SHAEF (the Allied headquarters). German occupying forces in the Netherlands surrendered formally on 5 May.

*Two civilians helping the security forces
to clear Brussels of German snipers in
September 1944.*

Belgium

In BELGIUM as in other European countries, the 1930s were an unhappy time. Belgium had been hard hit by the slump: unemployment rockcted upwards, and there was a succession of violent strikes in the coal-mining areas. Manufacturing declined drastically and exports fell by half between 1930 and 1932. On top of these economic problems, the febrile political situation threatened worse troubles ahead.

Following the sudden death of the beloved King Albert in 1934, Leopold III acceded to the throne. For several reasons, this was a more significant event than, for example, even the abdication of a monarch in Britain in 1936. In the first place, the Belgian monarchy in the 1930s possessed far greater constitutional powers than the British monarchy. At the same time, the symbolic significance of the monarch in Belgium was more important. Though a small nation, the Belgians are a divided nation — many of them would say they are not one single nation at all — and the king was a symbol of 'Belgianness', a quality otherwise rather hard to pin down.

Leopold III has been treated rather harshly by history. In 1934, though he could hardly be compared with the immensely popular Albert 'the Good', the personification of 'gallant little Belgium', he received a warm welcome from his subjects. A good deal of this, however, was due to the personality of his likeable Swedish-born queen, Astrid, who most unfortunately was killed in a motor accident less than two years later. Leopold subsequently made an unpopular morganatic second marriage, while officially a prisoner of war.

Leopold found the political waters muddy and storm-roughened. The coalition government was feeble and tottering towards resignation; the relatively new Socialist party was anxious to circumscribe the powers of the monarchy; the long-running hostility between Fleming and Walloon was sharper than ever; most sinister of all, there was a flourishing fascist party, the Rexists, who were particularly adept at stirring up scandals, real or invented, to embarrass the traditional political parties. In the general election of 1936, the Rexists won no less than 21 seats (in a house containing about 200 members), though they lost all but four in the 1939 election, when war seemed imminent. The foreign minister, Paul-Henri

Spaak, announced a new foreign policy, which he called 'independence-neutrality', which meant merely that Belgium, situated as she was in the 'cockpit of Europe', reserved the right to try to preserve herself by any feasible diplomatic means, and tacitly recognized the uselessness of the Locarno Pact or the League of Nations. In spite of some improvements in weaponry and the creation of a new frontier defence force, there was obviously little hope of Belgium long resisting a German attack. Along with other similarly plaintive voices Spaak was heard to say, 'Belgium has no ambition to be other than she is; she is searching for nothing and she asks for nothing – other than peace.' A request that was to be denied her. In the summer of 1939 some precautions were taken for war: the national bank made plans for the swift removal of its gold reserves, a food-rationing system was worked out, and the armed forces were part-mobilized. General mobilization began in August.

On the outbreak of war on 3 September, Belgium declared its neutrality in accordance with agreements made with Britain, France and Germany in 1937. In January 1940 a German aeroplane which made a forced landing on Belgian territory was found to contain plans for a German attack on the Anglo-French forces through Belgium. It was only a matter of time. The attack came at dawn on 10 May. The bulk of the Belgian air force was destroyed in a matter of hours; frontier strongholds which had been considered unconquerable fell almost as quickly, thanks, according to persistent though probably unreliable rumours, to traitors and fifth columnists. Chaos reigned, with thousands of refugees trying to get to France (there were nearly 50,000 Belgian-registered cars in the south of France in the summer of 1940). The refugees included by government direction all able-bodied young men not already in the armed forces. Movement was additionally hampered by a railway strike. Brussels fell on 18 May, but Leopold, as commander-in-chief of the Belgian forces, did not surrender until 28 May, when the Belgian army was in complete disarray and would hardly have held out a day longer. Having decided to surrender with his army, Leopold became a prisoner of war (though his 'prison' was the Château de Laeken). He refused to join the rest of the government in exile, at first in France, later in England. Although it must be said that most rulers who chose exile while their countries were occupied by the Axis had some difficulty in regaining their powers in 1945 (many never did), it was perhaps even less wise for Leopold to choose the role of defeated general surrendering with his troops. However correct his behaviour, he was bound to be suspected of collaboration. Due to faulty communications, moreover, his advice to the Allies of his impending surrender on 27 May had been held up, bringing unjust accusations of treachery upon his head. His role was compared very unfavourably with that of King Albert in 1914.

The Belgians had suffered over 12,000 casualties during the 18 days fighting, and were to suffer more in prison camps during the next five years (they also suffered over 6,000 civilians killed by Allied bombing in 1944).

But German occupation was not new to them; everyone over thirty remembered the four years of occupation during the Great War, 1914-18. There were some, indeed, who slipped quite easily into the same parts they had played in the earlier war. One man, Walthere Dewe, a fervent Catholic and devoted patriot, had run an intelligence network during the first war, and when the Germans arrived in 1940 he picked up his old contacts and soon had another network going. British Intelligence later dropped radio transmitters to him. Dewe was arrested in 1944 and shot while trying to escape.

Brussels, indeed, became a hotbed of espionage. It was the headquarters of the indestructible Leonid Trepper, who ran a famous underground organization for the benefit of the Soviet Union which was known as the Red Orchestra. Many books have been written about this network (including one by Trepper himself), and some authorities would say that its importance has been considerably overrated. It would be interesting to know the views of Soviet military intelligence.

As in other countries where the people were considered by racist dogma to be worth cultivating, in Belgium the Germans adopted at first a friendly stance. They were full of praise for the brave defence put up by the Belgian army, and perhaps contemplated the incorporation of Belgium, or part of it, in the Reich. Civilian resistance–unofficial civil-service go-slows, magistrates' refusals to carry out German orders, refusal of universities to submit lists of students for forced labour, general civilian disaffection– soon compelled the Germans to adopt a stricter role. Round-ups for the German labour camps increased tacit opposition and in turn provoked more brutal measures by the Gestapo.

The underground press had been vigorous during the German occupation in the Great War, and during the first six months of the second German occupation some 80 or 90 secret periodicals appeared. At one time in 1943 there were as many as 200 in circulation, though it should be emphasized that most of them were extremely short-lived and that the great majority had a print run of only a hundred or so copies.

Among the most famous and successful of Belgian resistance operations were the escape routes, mainly for Allied prisoners of war on the run or for downed Allied airmen evading capture, via various roundabout routes back to England. Some of these routes were extraordinarily elaborate, and the people who ran them, who came from all strata of society, displayed remarkable bravery and ingenuity. Many books have been written about the de Jonghs and other families who were engaged in this type of nerve-shattering activity (one example: Airey Neave, *Saturday at MI9*, London 1969), and their exploits have also given rise to a popular British television series (*The Secret Army*, 1977). Besides Allied personnel, many Belgians also managed to slip away to join the war against Hitler being directed from England, or to return equally secretly to co-ordinate resistance activities under the occupation. (The casualty rate for agents was high: of

Above: The German invasion of Belgium led to a mass exodus of civilian refugees to France.

Below: Leopold III (centre), in Switzerland shortly before his return from exile in 1950.

Above: A young man being searched by the Brussels police in April 1944 when sabotage was at its peak.

Below: The Belgian population gave an enthusiastic reception to the Allied forces in 1944.

250 agents who went from Britain into Belgium 105 were arrested; more than half of those were shot or died in captivity.)

The Belgians were somewhat less successful at hiding the Jews. Nearly 30,000 Jews were deported from Belgium by the Germans, and very few of them were ever seen again. However, it should be added that the great majority of these were political refugees from Germany who had only been in Belgium for at most six or seven years. Of Belgian-born Jews, comparatively few were deported to the camps, and there are many stories of acts of kindness and bravery by non-Jewish Belgians on behalf of their Jewish countrymen.

Belgium is topographically hardly more suitable than the Netherlands for guerrilla warfare (except of the modern, urban kind), the only region offering the requisite type of cover being the wooded Ardennes. Nevertheless there were many more or less militant resistance organizations in the country–too many in fact (at least a dozen of significant size) for really efficient operations. Corresponding to the Dutch *Orde Dienst* was the *Légion Belge*, dominated by army officers and intent not on fighting the Germans but on preserving the pre-war status quo and, by implication, preventing revolution and disorder. The *Légion Belge* nevertheless found relations with the Belgian government in exile, itself much damaged by feuds and conflict, less than amiable. A complication was the position of King Leopold, whom the British, no doubt wrongly, tended to regard as little better than a traitor (so, however, did a great many of his subjects). In 1943 the London-based government ordered the conversion of the *Légion* into the *Armée Secrète*, a force of 50,000 people, ultimately to come under Allied command when the day of liberation came.

On the far side of the political spectrum was the *Front de l'Indépendance*, Communist-dominated though including many non-Communists, especially young people. It was the most active of the Belgian resistance organizations, with a number of sabotage groups and a 'partisan army', so-called. It was also responsible for civil resistance– strikes, propaganda, etc., and ran a lively underground press. All resistance groups acknowledged the exiled government which, in co-operation with SOE and other Allied agencies, maintained relatively close control. Among the various militant underground groups there was, at times, a good deal of rivalry, much of it stemming from the need for weapons, which were mainly supplied by the British. Arms were in short supply, there was little actual fighting in Belgium anyway, and it was impossible to keep everyone happy.

In every country occupied by the Germans during the Second World War there were those who were ready to welcome the invaders and embraced their ideas and aims. Belgium had no Quisling–it was under German military government from the first–but it did have collaborationists. While it would be unfair, and probably untrue, to say that it had a relatively larger share of collaborators than other countries, certain features characteristic of Belgium made collaboration somewhat more significant. In particular, many Flemish nationalists looked hopefully towards Germany which, during the Great War, had recognised Flanders as to a degree separate. The Germans had accepted a Council of Flanders as a kind of semi-independent government in 1917, though they had not allowed complete separation. Flemish separation did not die in 1918. In the Belgian election of 1929 the Flemish nationalists won nine seats, and compelled the Belgian government to pay greater attention to the hitherto disregarded Flemings (for example, Flemish became an official language along with French for the first time). During the 1930s the Flemish nationalist movement showed a tendency to break up into small parties, several of which were blatantly fascist in character.

None of these movements, however, was as large as that of the Rexists, primarily a Walloon (French-speaking) movement, which as mentioned above acquired impressive though short-lived representation in parliament.

In the civil service, the Germans introduced men amenable to themselves by the simple step of lowering the retiring age by five years, which skimmed off the occupants of most of the top posts. These had acquired particular importance since the departure of the ministerial government. The new men were mainly members of a Flemish nationalist fascist party (the Flemings were naturally more attractive to the Nazis than the Walloons), but the Rexists were not far behind.

There were collaborators active in other fields, for example the press, and a Walloon and a Flemish SS unit were formed which attracted about 4,000 recruits. Some units fought for the Germans in Russia. They suffered heavy casualties, but then collaborationists at home were far from safe either, due to some expert assassinations carried out by the resistance. Moreover, after the war, collaborationists were pursued more vigorously than anywhere except Norway. In the words of the Rexist leader, as he set out for the Russian front, 'We go forth slandered, misunderstood, even hated' (quoted by David Littlejohn, *The Patriotic Traitors*, London 1972).

The Secret Army was prepared to rise up against the Germans to assist in the liberation of Belgium, but as things turned out the Allied armies moved so rapidly that no rising was necessary. (Eisenhower was also anxious to prevent a premature rising and resulting massacre, as happened in other places.) Nevertheless, the various underground organizations in Belgium, partisan groups in the Ardennes (who had proved useful in cleaning-up operations after the Ardennes offensive) as well as resistance workers in the cities, played a valuable role in the closing stages of the war. The Secret Army carried out a particularly skilful operation in Antwerp (a hotbed of Flemish fascism, incidentally) where, with the aid of a rapid British push, it helped to secure the port almost undamaged for the Allies notwithstanding well-laid German plans to destroy all the harbour installations.

*A member of the Maquis on guard duty
in the Haute Loire region.*

France

WHEN FRANCE AND BRITAIN declared war on Germany in September 1939, there appeared to be no cause for pessimism regarding the outcome. The French army was held in high repute, not only by its own officers but by many others inside and outside France, including Winston Churchill. The Maginot Line, the defence works built specifically against German attack, was universally believed to be impregnable (as it probably was; unfortunately, the Germans, when the time came, elected to go around it). The resources of the British Empire appeared to provide a reserve of strength which would eventually prove too much even for Germany. Indeed, the French government acted during the first six months of the war as though the chief enemies of France were not the Germans outside but the Communists within. The seventy Communist deputies in the French Assembly were ejected from their seats, and thousands of people in the provinces were arrested or removed from office. At the same time, aggressive motions towards Germany were discouraged, and nothing was done to disturb the peculiar calm of the *drôle de guerre* for fear of provoking Germany.

In May 1940 the calm was shattered as Germany began its major offensive in the west. Belgium and the Netherlands were swiftly overrun. The Anglo-French forces were split apart, and the British Expeditionary Force, plus a few French troops, scrambled to safety across the Channel from Dunkirk. A second German thrust penetrated deep into France and, during the first week of June, the French forces crumbled like stale cake. The Italians joined in the attack just in time to snatch at Savoy and the French Riviera. There was, in France, something approaching total moral as well as military collapse: the will to resist was just not there. Why this happened (and a vast number of reasons and explanations have been put forward) can probably never be fully understood, and in the present context the question is relevant only insofar as the military collapse did little, initially, to encourage resistance to the conquerors.

According to the terms of the armistice, France was divided into two zones. Marshal Philippe Pétain, the aged hero of the First World War, was installed as head of a truncated state in the south and west with the seat of government at the spa town of Vichy. The Germans in theory played no role in the Vichy state, although in fact the *Abwehr* (military intelligence) and other units, such as those hunting illegal radio transmitters, had complete freedom of action. The motto of Pétain's regime was *Travail, Famille, Patrie* ('Work, Family, Nation'), of which there were many sardonic parodies (e.g. *Trahison, Famine, Prison*, 'Treason, Famine, Prison'), while de Gaulle's response was 'Work? He lost the habit long ago. Family? He's an old libertine. Nation? The saviour of Verdun turned traitor.' The remainder of France, including Paris and the whole of the Atlantic coast, came under German occupation.

There were, naturally, many different views on what the attitude of Frenchmen should be towards their conquerors – and towards the Vichy government. Some favoured full co-operation with the Germans in creating the European 'New Order'. A large number believed in 'making the best of it' – being reasonably friendly towards the Germans and trying to do as much as possible in the interests of France by open bargaining and persuasion. Some 3,000 Frenchmen fought more or less enthusiastically with the Germans on the Eastern Front. A considerably larger number volunteered to serve in the Waffen SS when racial restrictions were sufficiently relaxed to allow non-Aryans to become members of that organization. It was not difficult to find willing recruits for the *Milice Française*, Joseph Darnand's anti-resistance militia, formed in 1943 and hated, if possible, more than the Gestapo itself. As well as these there were hundreds of thousands of passive collaborators.

Besides those who preferred co-operation with the Germans, whole-hearted or not, there were many who advocated outright resistance. Their motives were almost as various as their faces or fingerprints: patriotism, a love of adventure, these were often decisive; while other people were for one reason or another forced to join the resistance in order to elude the authorities. There were nationalists of the fairly far right, and there were members of groups still farther to the left. Some were Communists already on the run from the French government before the invasion, although the main Communist effort in the resistance did not come until after Germany's attack on the Soviet Union.

Some French people refused to accept the Armistice and fled the country before the Germans took over. Among them was General Charles de Gaulle, who arrived in London alone, penniless, without friends and without any authority. He was, nevertheless, not totally unknown, and had briefly held the post of under-secretary for war before his flight to London. Fortunately for himself and for France, de Gaulle appealed to Churchill, who saw him as the man around whom the French might rally and gave him invaluable access to the air waves. On 18 June de Gaulle made his famous first broadcast from London, calling on the French to continue the fight (although no recording of the broadcast exists, his famous remark that France had lost a battle but had not lost the war was first made on a later occasion). De Gaulle searched sincerely for some figure more substantial than himself to take over leadership of the 'Free French' (or, as Churchill preferred, the 'Fighting French'), but he received little support; even the French embassy staff in London, with one exception, chose to return to Pétain's France. On 26 June therefore, the British government recognized de Gaulle as 'chief of all the Free French, wherever they might be'. This Churchill did not achieve without opposition. The Foreign Office correctly pointed out that it would inevitably lead to political difficulties, and the Americans, prone to favour Vichy, did not like it; but Churchill, a greater Francophile than de Gaulle was an Anglophile, had spotted the man's potential.

During the summer of 1940, the situation of the headquarters of the Free French in London was, perhaps understandably, chaotic. Apart from political and personal conflicts and rivalries, aggravated by much intelligence and counter-intelligence shenanigans, there was at first a desperate shortage of staff. De Gaulle himself was usually out of the office at various meetings, making contacts and enforcing hard bargains (he decided that since he had no military 'punch', obstinacy was his best weapon) and his ADC was also often called away. There were virtually no other staff, and according to one story a well-known left-wing journalist who called at the office to ask if he could enrol with the Free French found himself signed on immediately and asked to take charge of the premises for the afternoon.

De Gaulle's efforts to build up his authority from the very fragile base on which he started received a near-disastrous setback from the unhappy episode of Mers-el-Kebir, when the British attacked the French fleet in North Africa to preclude the possibility of its falling into German control. Soon afterwards, however, his status was much enhanced when most of French Equatorial Africa embraced his cause, and he set off on a triumphant tour of those provinces, marred only slightly by the failure to capture the French West African port of Dakar on the way.

De Gaulle was a professional soldier and, at first, he saw little purpose in the French resistance except for its intelligence potential. Moreover, de Gaulle was no politician–at least in the sense of party politics. He naturally had little sympathy with the revolutionary aspect of the Resistance, which grew increasingly pronounced from 1941. Yet he managed to draw in men of every political persuasion, men like the Socialist Pierre Brossolette (who was to throw himself from a Gestapo fifth-floor window rather than risk giving up secrets under torture) and, after the PCF (French Communist Party) had given him its allegiance in January 1943, the Communist Fernand Grenier, who became a close colleague though they quarrelled later. In fact de Gaulle was, in a wider sense, an excellent politician, and certainly more flexible than he has often been painted. Otherwise he would hardly have been able to set up successfully the CLNF (National Committee of Liberation) in June 1943, which was for all practical purposes a provisional government, and to circumvent the revolution desired by the Communists.

The Gaullist agency in touch with the resistance in France was the BCRA (*Bureau Central de Renseignements et d'Action*), which was, to de Gaulle's irritation, under the general control of the British SOE though operating to a large extent independently. Although at first, and under a different name, concerned almost exclusively with intelligence, it came to adopt a much wider role. What was even more trying to the French in London was that they had no control at all in SOE's affairs, and SOE not infrequently kept them in the dark about operations of which they felt they should have been advised beforehand. The British, after Dakar, never trusted Free French security.

Although it has been said that, in June 1940, 99 per cent of the French people accepted the German occupation and the Vichy regime (but also that 99 per cent rejected the Germans four years later), a number of resistance groups developed quite early. The Germans themselves were largely responsible, despite their initial front of benignity, for provoking many people into resistance. When the French saw food and machinery being packed up to be transported to Germany, when they had German soldiers billeted among them, saw German soldiers strutting about the streets and apparently enjoying themselves–in marked contrast to the local inhabitants–they began to think very unfriendly thoughts about their conquerors. At first their desire to get their own back was manifested in rather silly, but perhaps psychologically satisfying ways, misdirecting German drivers, selling them dud articles in the shops, failing to stop the train at a station where only Germans wished to alight, and so on. From there it was a short step to active resistance. The well-known resistance group associated with the Musée de l'Homme, which was in existence by the early autumn of 1940, grew out of a group of friends meeting regularly and discussing their wish to 'do something'. They attracted others; their membership covered a wide political spectrum (though not including Communists) and included people of many different occupations (though mainly middle-class). Its chief work was in helping escaped prisoners and others anxious to elude the Germans, and smuggling them out of occupied France; it also published one of the earliest underground newspapers. Like virtually all other networks of any size or longevity, it was not immune to the Germans. Seven members were executed and others imprisoned in early 1941, and the following November it was virtually destroyed in a Gestapo round-up as a result of which fourteen people were shot or otherwise killed by the Germans.

Active resistance developed first in the occupied zone. Under Vichy rule, the *attentiste* ('wait and see') attitude was more common. Pétain, after all, was a national hero, and his government was at least made up of Frenchmen, most of whom believed, if with less fiery conviction than de Gaulle, that they were doing the best thing for France. Resistance at first took the form of insult and criticism: it was possible still to be quite frank about the regime without running the risk of instant arrest. By and by more serious resistance was organized. The little groups which were eventually to come together to form the well-known network code-named *Combat* were organized during the summer and autumn of 1940.

There were soon a great number of resistance groups in the field. Some of them recognized de Gaulle; others were reluctant to do so. The task of uniting them was undertaken by Jean Moulin.

Moulin was one of the giants of the French resistance. When the Germans invaded he was, at 41, the youngest prefect in France. He remained at his post in Chartres (where today an impressive monument to his memory may be seen) but was quickly at odds with the Germans when they tried to make him sign a document in which atrocities committed by them were blamed on French troops. He was tortured, and tried to kill himself by cutting his throat. After a spell in hospital, he lost his official position and travelled to the south of France, where he made contact with many resistance groups including those which later fused to form *Combat*. On their behalf he travelled to London in October 1941 to have discussions with de Gaulle. He was in a position to make himself a major leader of the French against the Germans, but he chose to do so as the loyal subordinate of de Gaulle. With the New Year, Jean Moulin was parachuted back into France. During the following year and a half, he welded the main resistance groups into a single, Gaullist organization. It was a remarkable achievement.

Of course he had certain advantages. He had de Gaulle behind him for a start, and although that was not always an advantage, it meant that he was reasonably well provided with funds, and thus supplies, arms, ammunition. But his success resulted rather more from his own capacities. Hoarse-voiced, the legacy of his suicide attempt, he was an excellent negotiator – tactful, charming, quick-witted and, if necessary, tough. For more than a year he moved in the shifting, dangerous world of the Resistance, slowly and painfully pulling the threads together, gently persuading people who by the nature of their secret work were inevitably individualists by temperament and independents by preference, of the necessity for co-operation. He saw some networks ruined before his eyes as the Gestapo, like an avid cancer, fastened upon one small part and from there rapidly spread, until the whole body was infected and destroyed. But eventually he succeeded in uniting nearly the whole Resistance movement. The *Mouvements Unis de Résistance* (MUR, which also means 'wall') was originally created in the Vichy zone, and of course included *Combat* as well as other large organizations in the south. The predominantly (not exclusively) Communist *Front National* did not join at that time. The *Front National*, launched in May 1941 and inactive until the German invasion of Russia, was better organized thanks to the training and experience of its leaders. Constructed as a network of small cells with minimal contact between any two, it was less vulnerable to the kind of devastating round-up that often followed the smallest penetration of other networks. The various techniques of underground warfare were already well known, and they had been refined and improved by the experience of the Spanish Civil War. It was, however, more than a party organization, and included among its members many people, who were in no way Communist sympathizers. Later the *Front National* and its fighting off-shoot, the FTP (*Francs-tireurs et Partisans*), became less heterogeneous.

The attitude of the *Front National* to de Gaulle and the MUR was not unfriendly but aloof, though there were cases of co-operation at local level even while the Communists were officially steering clear of de Gaulle. At the same time, the MUR was not so firmly united as its name proclaimed, for the rivalries between the various groups composing it did not entirely cease with their unification. The 'Secret Army', which was the militant arm of the MUR formed out of a number of paramilitary organizations and intended to be the chief weapon in a future popular rising against the Germans, was commanded by a regular staff officer known to de Gaulle named General Charles Delestraint, and this appointment was by no means welcome to all the resistance leaders on the spot, while in London many people viewed the centralizing tendency of resistance—perhaps necessary to assert de Gaulle's authority—with misgivings.

However, there was something to be said for creating a division between civilian and military resistance. Specialization was inevitable, and from the early days groups like *Combat* had included paramilitary units—'shock troops'—numbering about 30 men which, like the specialized sabotage groups that were also created, played no active role immediately but were seen rather as an investment for the future. 'Resistance' of course, includes any number of activities—forging documents, printing underground propaganda, organizing escapes, acquiring intelligence, etc.—and there are literally thousands of books describing these and other underground activities in occupied France. Most people involved were only part-time resistance workers, who had ordinary jobs and led normal family lives for 90 per cent of the time, though there were many full-time agents also.

With the aid of other agents, such as Pierre Brossolette and Wing Commander F. F. E. Yeo-Thomas ('the White Rabbit') Moulin created in 1943 the *Conseil National de la Résistance* (CNR), a national organization including political, religious and social leaders in France, committed to de Gaulle and opposed to the Germans and Vichy (by that time also under direct German occupation). It included members of the old political parties of the Third Republic, in spite of the almost universal agreement of the French people that the Third Republic was utterly discredited and the particular resentment of resistance leaders. De Gaulle himself had once spoken over the radio of a 'revolution' in preparation by those engaged in resistance; but he needed to buttress his own position with the old Third Republic politicians, especially in view of the partiality being shown at this time by the Americans and the British for his rival, General Henri Giraud, recently escaped from German captivity and currently established in North Africa as co-leader of Free France.

The CNR first met in Paris in May 1943. It was in fact its only full meeting until after the liberation. Moulin himself was arrested less than two months later, through treachery. The Gestapo killed him slowly, but he told them nothing. Formation of the CNR was a lengthy and difficult business. The attitude of de Gaulle himself was not always helpful. He believed in compensating for the essential weakness of his position by a corresponding display of belligerence, tactics very irritating to colleagues such as Churchill and Roosevelt, and his tendency to assume without question that he was the true leader of the resistance whom all ought to obey was often resented in France. Many local resistance leaders had barely heard of de Gaulle before his broadcast from London, and suspected that he was a puppet of the British, who could not be trusted since the British were not supplying them with all the arms and explosives they wanted—the perennial complaint of guerrillas.

The CNR meeting in May 1943 passed unanimously (though after some argument from Communist representatives) a resolution declaring null and void the authority of Vichy and acknowledging de Gaulle as trustee of the interests of France. De Gaulle did not control the CNR, of course, though his delegate (Moulin had four successors within one year) was an important influence. It was, in effect, an independent body, and it set up a number of 'Liberation Committees' around the country which were Communist-dominated. However, it did not get around to publishing its full political programme until shortly before the liberation.

In 1942 the shortage of manpower was beginning to seem Germany's greatest problem. The Russian front, like some insatiable maw, sucked in men by the thousand. The factories had to be emptied to man the regiments, and Germany was increasingly compelled to draw on the resources of the occupied countries to fulfil its labour needs. At first various volunteer schemes were introduced, often accompanied by quite attractive inducements. Such schemes had only limited success; they certainly did not solve the problem. The Germans next turned to coercion, and in France the compulsory labour service was introduced in February 1943. While it may have increased the supply of labour flowing from France into Germany for a short time, it is at least arguable that the policy was a mistake because of its psychological effect on the French. People were appalled at the sudden round-ups of young able-bodied men, the sweeps through factories and villages, the threats of reprisals against the families of those who tried to dodge the labour draft. In particular, the peasant class, until then fairly complacent about the occupation and, in many cases, making a fine profit from selling farm products on the black market, turned against the Germans. The sons of peasant families themselves joined the Maquis (the spontaneous underground army) to avoid the draft, thus helping to make the Maquis more acceptable to ordinary country people. Those who previously might have been indifferent, to say the least, towards Jews in hiding, prisoners escaping, or resisters planning sabotage, adopted a more benign attitude. The oppressive labour dictate united all classes in opposition to the occupying powers and created a feeling of brotherhood among the people.

The Resistance in Paris helped to sabotage the forced-labour schemes. A train was scheduled to leave the Gare de L'Est in October 1942 with 400 'relief workers' bound for Germany. A ceremony had been planned, with speeches and brass band, but unfortunately for the organizers, only 27 out of the expected 400 men appeared at the station, which rather spoiled the effect. Nevertheless, the speeches were made, the band played, and at last the whistle blew. The engine puffed slowly away from the platform, but the carriages remained at rest, someone having uncoupled them.

Although the compulsory labour service was the chief reason for the rapidly expanding numbers of people involved in some form of resistance from 1943 onwards, there were other motives at work. It was steadily becoming apparent to most people that sooner or later (and it was beginning to look sooner) the Germans were going to lose the war. No one likes being on the losing side, and many Frenchmen began to look ahead and wonder what they would answer when their children asked them what they did in the war. (In 1945, it was extremely difficult to find anyone who had not, according to his own account, done something in the Resistance). Alongside this fear of being identified with the Germans after the war, many people feared the Allies, feared the propaganda promises of what would happen to collaborators after the war, even feared the effects of Allied warfare–the giant bombing raids–and perhaps hoped to avoid destruction by friendly powers in the air by performing their job for them on the ground.

But how did one join the Resistance? One could not merely declare that one had done so and carry on as before. It was necessary to go 'underground', and that meant becoming, so far as the authorities were concerned, a non-person, foregoing, for example, ration cards and similar– otherwise desirable–means of identification. It was impossible for the towns to support a large clandestine population, even if the cover were available, and it was therefore necessary for the great majority of those who 'dropped out' in order to avoid labour service in Germany to go to the country. Between February 1943 and June 1944 about 100,000 men disappeared for this reason, many of them accompanied by their families.

Resistance organizations and the trade unions did what they could to help these people. The CNR set up various committees specifically to deal with the problems of those joining the Maquis to avoid the labour draft; but money, the most necessary commodity in the circumstances, was in short supply. Some was sent by BCRA; some from other British sources; some was raised in one way or another by the Resistance themselves. But

Top: De Gaulle inspired much of the resistance movement but never won the undivided loyalty of the Maquis.

Above left: Jean Moulin, Prefect of Chartres before the war, was de Gaulle's representative in France from 1941.

Above right: Wing-Commander Yeo-Thomas, the 'White Rabbit', a brilliant SOE agent who worked in the Angoulême and Lyons areas.

Above: French workers leaving for workcamps in Germany with pro-Vichy slogans chalked on the carriage.

Below: The Maquis in the Haute Loire were well equipped with weapons and uniforms.

Above: Civilian clothes were inadequate for the new life of men who went underground.

Below: A group of the Maquis in Corsica training with weapons dropped to them by the Allies.

the total was far from adequate. The Communists were very active in this work; they were of course strong in French industry, and their reward was the growing strength of their party in the Resistance also.

Much ingenuity was displayed in the forging of documents; one oft-repeated story relates how the Resistance, to compensate for the imperfections of their forged and very numerous ration cards, successfully spread a rumour that the *real* cards were forgeries. Food and clothing were less easily supplied. Many new recruits to the Maquis had left their homes or jobs at short notice, bringing nothing with them but the clothes they stood up in and even those were often of little use, for a city suit is not an ideal garment for living rough in the mountains. The authorities, and all those who were opposed to the resistance, loudly broadcast news of robberies with violence by which the Maquis acquired food, clothing and other essentials. Much of this was propaganda of course, but no one seriously denies that such incidents did take place.

One Maquis instruction for potential recruits advised them to bring warm clothes, hobnailed boots, and a set of identity papers and ration card, forged or genuine. It warned that the Maquis lived poorly: food was often hard to find and contact with families was strictly forbidden. Sometimes food was 'bought' for credit, but the notes given in exchange for goods were dubious and the vendor was well aware that the chances of such notes ever being redeemed were slim (though some were).

By the end of 1943 fairly large sums of money were reaching the Maquis from London, but divided up among individuals the cash did not go far. Sympathizers might provide cash, or food, or medicine, and although it is often said, not only by Communists, that the richer classes in occupied France contributed little to resistance funds, the banks willy-nilly provided a good deal. Bank robbery by resistance groups became a frequent source of supply, and in many cases was made easier by the co-operation of members of the bank staff. Similarly, hospital staff sometimes made it easy for the Maquis to steal medical supplies.

But a shortage more desperate than food or medicine was arms. The small arms not surrendered at the armistice mostly fell into German hands eventually, though the Resistance got hold of some, and of some Italian weapons when Italy surrendered to the Allies. Arms of a kind – various explosive devices mainly – were manufactured by the Resistance, but the main source of arms and ammunition was, inevitably, Britain, and although numerous parachute drops of weapons were made to various groups in different parts of France, supply never came anywhere near satisfying demand until very late in the day. It was widely believed that the poor supply owed something to British fears of Communist influence in the Resistance, but the known facts suggest that French resistance groups were not deliberately starved of arms for political reasons. In the early years, there was a general shortage of arms, and naturally regular troops had to be equipped first. There was never much likelihood of the Allies supplying the weaponry and vehicles that the Maquis wanted until the invasion of France was imminent. Apart from those few organizations directly concerned with irregular warfare in occupied Europe, the attitude of Allied command towards the Resistance was in general *attentiste*.

The word *maquis* comes from the name of the dense scrub of mountainous Corsica, where outlaws and bandits would hide out from the authorities. It was in Corsica that the Resistance achieved one of its most striking early successes. Corsica was occupied by the Italians after the Allied invasion of North Africa in November 1942 but, largely as a result of successful operations by the Italian secret police, the Resistance was not particularly strong there, except among the Communists: the *Front National* could call on several thousand men. As the surrender of the Italians began to appear inevitable, the numbers increased. Moreover, it seemed likely that at that time the majority of Italian troops would be inclined to side with the Resistance against the Germans. When the day of surrender came, the Resistance therefore attacked only the 10,000-odd German troops, and in general the Italians fought with the Resistance. Thus the port of Bastia, which changed hands more than once in the few days of fighting, was gained by the Free French, as they now declared themselves, with the aid of the troops who had formed the garrison of the town during the Italian occupation. However, the Germans, reinforced from Sardinia, were soon able to retake the port.

Even with Italian assistance, the Corsicans could hardly hope to resist a determined German counter-attack without the heavy weapons that only the Allies could provide. These appeared not to be forthcoming. In fact the Resistance in Corsica had maintained only sporadic contact with London, and de Gaulle's chief agent, Captain Fred Scamaroni, had been captured by the Italians in late 1942 and subsequently killed. The Resistance was in closer touch with General Giraud's headquarters in Algiers, through the military intelligence system Giraud inherited from Admiral Darlan; but there was not a great deal that Giraud could do. Some arms were brought in secretly before the rising started, by British submarine; a French submarine brought in about one hundred men, and a couple of overloaded motor torpedo boats landed a battalion with its invaluable artillery. Some belated air support was provided by the Americans from North African airfields, and de Gaulle, who had not been informed of Giraud's dealings with the Corsican Resistance until a very late stage (a lapse which, incidentally, provoked his successful coup against Giraud) sent troops while the rising was in progress, and was able to check the Communist takeover of communications and local government which was proceeding along with liberation. A month after the announcement of the Italian surrender, Corsica was freed. A German force which in total numbered close to 40,000 men had been defeated (though most got away safely), and the chief agents of the victory were the Corsican Resistance, mainly the *Francs-tireurs et Partisans*..

The Maquis included others besides ordinary Frenchmen seeking to avoid the labour draft. There were many Jews, not surprisingly, and also a number of Dutch, Belgians, Poles and Yugoslavs. There were refugees from Alsace and Lorraine who, whatever the Germans believed, thought of themselves as French and not German; there were some escaped Russian prisoners of war, and there were even a few Germans, anti-Nazi deserters from the Wehrmacht. Some of the most effective of all fighters against the German occupation of France were Spanish republicans, refugees from Franco, who were politically committed, experienced in guerrilla warfare, and had little to lose.

Estimates of the numbers of the Maquis vary considerably, not only because it is difficult to estimate the actual numbers but also because of doubts over exactly who should be counted. In spite of several well-known large formations, most Maquis groups were small and poorly armed. They suffered heavy casualties to the Germans and the Vichy police, and they could only survive in areas which were either forested or mountainous, preferably both. The earliest groups could be found in late 1940 in Alpine districts, and by early 1943 there were a large number scattered about the Massif Central. There were almost none in the comparatively unsheltered north until 1944. But by the spring of that year the total number of the Maquis was probably over 50,000. A year earlier the total had been little more than half that.

The Maquis, growing up to a large extent unasked and unplanned, presented a major problem for the Resistance. The Secret Army, like similar organizations in other occupied countries, was an army in theory only. It did not actually parade, fight battles, or even draw regular pay. The Maquis, on the other hand, if it was to be anything, had to be a real army. This was generally recognized, and both MUR and the Communists worked to turn the Maquis into a fighting arm of the Free French.

There were, however, differing opinions on how such an irregular army should be organized. What, for example, was the ideal size for a guerrilla unit? Most units were not more than twenty, thirty, or forty men, but some numbered several hundreds, a few over a thousand. A unit of such a size, however, sacrificed some of the advantages of guerrilla war, notably ease of mobility. The Vercors disaster cruelly illustrated this liability.

The Vecors, near Grenoble in the south-east of France, has the look of a fortress built by nature. It is a spade-shaped, high plateau about 50 km from north to south and 25 km from east to west. It is bounded by the rivers Drôme, Isère and Drac, tributaries of the Rhône, and superficially it appears excellent territory for guerrilla war, being mountainous, part forested, and topographically complex, with many valleys, cliffs and peaks. True, it has half a dozen roads and a dozen or more trails lacing through it, and it has one weak point above Grenoble, where access to the centre of the plateau may be gained by a broad sloping valley that breaches the natural ramparts. However, a small number of sharpshooters ought to be able to hold the district against vastly greater regular forces.

So at least it seemed to General Delestraint, commander of the Secret Army. Early in 1943, Delestraint, in London for a conference with de Gaulle's staff, presented a plan for holding the Vecors as a knife in the enemy's back in the event of Allied landings in the south of France. The originator of the plan was a local architect, Pierre Dalloz, and the Vercors already held a considerable number of *maquisards*, much reinforced in the previous few months following the dissolution of the 'Armistice Army' of Vichy.

The plan was apparently accepted in London, though it later turned out that key people remained ignorant of it. In April 1943, Delestraint visited the Vercors to make tactical preparations for the revolt, code-named Operation Montagnards, which, the more hopeful believed, might be required at any moment. But the next few months brought only setbacks. Delestraint was arrested by the Germans and sent to a concentration camp (he was shot two years later). Several leading *maquisards* of the Vercors were captured by the Italians, and numbers declined. Nevertheless, the plan was not abandoned, and Pierre Dalloz took a trip by hedge-hopping Lysander to London to discuss details. There, however, he became a pawn of political and personal rivalries, and the plan remained unconsidered by those whose co-operation was vital.

The Vercors had begun as a refuge for those seeking to avoid the enemy rather than to engage him, but in the course of 1943 it became a major base for Maquis raids. Some of these were quite serious: a munitions dump in Grenoble was destroyed in one raid, and in another several German vehicles were captured. These raids were supported by arms drops from Allied aircraft.

In January 1944 the Germans attacked the Vercors in force from Grenoble. They burned several houses, in one case with eight people inside, and destroyed a couple of hamlets. There were a few casualties on both sides, but the most important aspect of the German attack as an episode in irregular warfare was that it showed how a strong redoubt can become a menace to its defenders when it is attacked by a superior force of regular troops. Further punitive expeditions by the Germans in March and April emphasized this lesson which, however, was not taken to heart.

Without entering the tangled labyrinths of French and Allied headquarters in Algiers and London (where the plan for Operation Montagnards was apparently put into a 'pending' tray and completely forgotten for over six months), it is necessary only to say that liaison with the Vercors was poor, and it was perhaps not surprising that when, on the eve of D-Day, the call came from London for the Resistance to launch its long-planned campaign of disruption, the Maquis in the Vercors took it as their signal to rise. They did not realize that the basic conditions for their rising did not exist: no major Allied landing was about to take place *in the south of France* to engage the main force of the Germans in their region;

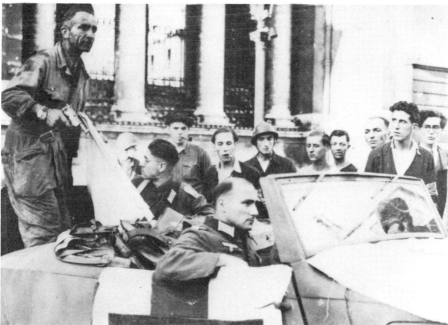

Opposite above: Attacks on trains were some of the most important operations of the French Resistance.

Below: Two women mourning for one of the victims of the massacre at Oradour in 1944.

Top: A girl member of the Resistance in action in the streets of Paris in August 1944.

Above: German officers being driven away under guard after the surrender of Paris in August 1944.

there had been no co-ordinated endorsement of the plan by Algiers and London, and therefore the heavy air support that was expected and needed was by no means assured.

By the time serious fighting began on 13 June, there were about 3,000 Frenchmen in the Vercors, though not all of them were armed – or armed adequately. The Germans were able to call on about four times as many, all well-armed professionals, backed up by aircraft and artillery. The Maquis were not worried by the odds; they had anticipated them. Nor were they greatly concerned at their own lack of artillery and air support, as they expected these deficiencies to be rapidly made good. Moreover, like the Home Army in Warsaw, they expected to fight for only a few days, until they were overrun by friendly regular forces.

It was a fine, warm day. The Germans advanced up the valley from Grenoble and attacked St Nizier. They met fierce resistance from a much smaller number of defending *maquisards*, and the same evening they retired, having suffered about sixty casualties to the French ten. Clearly, resistance was stiffer than they had expected, and they laid down a hefty artillery barrage before they renewed their attack, this time in much larger numbers.

The French could not hold the Germans off for long. Although aircraft from Algiers had dropped a few weapons, the Maquis still had nothing more potent than hand grenades or bazookas. They fell back and the Germans, setting a standard of brutality which was to be one of the characteristics of the Vercors battle, burned St Nizier stick and stone, tossing the bodies of their dead enemies on to the blaze.

However, the Germans did not follow up this initial success as quickly as might have been expected. The Maquis consolidated in the southern half of the Vercors, receiving almost daily new recruits and parachuted arms. The 'Republic of Vercors' enjoyed its brief, fantastic spell of liberty (with a surprisingly sophisticated civil administration), and received messages of congratulation from London and elsewhere. An American team of specialists was parachuted in, closely followed by 'Eucalyptus' – a team of Allied officers of various nationalities not all of whom could speak French very well. A French group arrived from Algiers to prepare an airstrip on the plateau. This was the most encouraging development yet; para-troopers were expected at any moment. A huge force of US bombers droned over, dropping their supplies, but when they had gone the skies echoed with a less welcome noise as German bombers attempted to flatten the villages of the Vercors.

Still the airborne troops did not come, and on 19 July the Germans began a new attack in overwhelming force. The whole area was surrounded and cut off. The ramparts were forced, and the defenders fell back. The fine weather had passed. Rain began to fall heavily.

Just as things were beginning to look really grim, the sound of engines was heard, and twenty aircraft appeared in the distance towing gliders.

They landed on the airstrip newly prepared for the American Dakotas. But these were not Dakotas, and the troops inside them were not Allied troops. They were Waffen-SS. Most of the defenders were wiped out before they had recovered from their surprise. The French launched a desperate counter-attack against the enemy in their midst, but they were beaten off as more German aeroplanes arrived and the Germans extended their foothold. All civilians in their sector were killed, some in horribly savage ways. Houses were set on fire and the inmates, including children, shot as they dashed out.

It was all over quite quickly. Some desperate rearguard actions were fought by small groups and individuals, as the Germans blasted through the Vercors. One party of seventeen men, crossing from one pass to another, was caught in German fire in an unsheltered position between the two. They managed to slide down a rock face and tumbled into a convenient cave, where they were pinned down by about one hundred Germans on the heights of both sides of the little valley where they were trapped. Night came and there was silence. Gingerly, one of the Frenchmen threw out a stone to see if the enemy had gone. Tracers, flares, grenades and machine-gun fire assured him they had not. The machine guns could not get an angle to fire into the cave, so next morning the Germans rushed it with grenades. The defenders picked up the grenades and hurled them back, and although one Frenchman was killed, there were more German casualties than French. Next the Germans tried lowering a bomb on a string from above, but a Frenchman grabbed it, cut the string, and threw the bomb away. They tried again, jerking the bomb up and down, and this time it exploded in the mouth of the cave, but without causing any casualties. On the second night, the men inside decided to make a break for safety. By lucky chance it was foggy, and the German flares made little impression on the Alpine mist. The little group of Frenchmen raced along the valley, up the gentler slope at the end, and over the top to safety.

Other little actions usually ended less happily for the French. Although a good number of fighting men did manage to escape through the German lines, those who did not, including the old, the sick, and the young, were massacred. Total casualties were close to one thousand. The French commander, Colonel Huet, signalled London at the end: 'We are bitter at being abandoned, alone and without support in the hour of battle.'

How many brave fighters there were, in that war, who felt themselves betrayed by their own side, when vital support which had been promised, or they believed had been promised, failed to arrive. The feelings of the survivors of the Vercors are understandable, but the plain, cruel fact is that the Vercors operation was an almost certain disaster from the word go. Some people had even said it would be.

There were long arguments about how resistance generally should be organized for the final ejection of the Germans. It was agreed early in 1944 that the Maquis and the Secret Army should be incorporated in the FFI

(*Forces Françaises de l'Interieur*) from D-Day onwards. In a sense, therefore, the Maquis ceased to exist on the day the Allied forces landed.

To speak of 'the Maquis' or indeed 'the Resistance' generally gives a false sense of homogeneity. They included many organizations and many individuals of widely differing ideas and intentions. Even in the Maquis there were many who were opposed to provocative action against the Germans (at least as long as there was any danger of reprisals). As elsewhere, the Communists were among the most militant. London and Algiers did not encourage active operations which were considered likely to do more harm than good, and in fact most of the direct fighting between the Maquis and the Germans, until the eve of the invasion of Normandy, was not started by the Maquis. What frequently happened was that the *Milice* or some other collaborationist force decided on a 'sweep' against the Maquis, found they had bitten off more than they could chew, and were forced to call in the German forces to complete the job. That was more or less what happened at Glières in March 1944.

Some 500 *maquisards* had held out successfully in the snow at Glières against the *Milice* since the beginning of the year, when the Germans moved in. There were about 8,000 German troops, in their white mountain battle dress, and they were supported by artillery and aircraft. The Maquis had nothing much heavier than British machine guns and mortars. Though the Maquis managed to fight them off for a few days, they were obviously outclassed and were eventually forced to break off and disperse. They lost about 150 men – the Germans killed all the wounded they found – but the rest slipped away safely through mountain passes.

Throughout the summer of 1944 France was seething with guerrilla warfare. A number of little 'republics', like the Vercors, appeared triumphantly declaring their freedom, only to be suppressed again by the Germans or quietly reorganized by advancing Gaullist forces. But in France as elsewhere, guerrilla warfare as such was of dubious value. The kind of militant resistance likely to be more productive was sabotage.

Regular army officers tend inevitably to look down on irregulars, and headquarters commands are inclined to place a rather low value on operations by resistance workers and partisans. Early attempts to put regular officers in command of Maquis were (with some exceptions) unsuccessful not only because such commanders were not welcome to the *maquisards* but also because many army officers did not much fancy the idea of commanding a small and ill-armed rabble in the forests, or preferred Pétain to de Gaulle. Similarly, Allied command was inclined to prefer orthodox methods of warfare to unorthodox; to favour bombers rather than saboteurs.

Harry Rée, an SOE agent in France, now better known as an educationalist, has recounted one story in support of sabotage against the bomber ('Agents, Resisters and the Local Population', in Hawes and White, *Resistance in Europe*, London 1975).

In July 1943 it was decided that the Peugeot factory in Montbéliard, which had been converted to make tank parts for Germany, should be put out of action; accordingly the RAF despatched their bombers. Much damage was done in the town, and in Besançon not far away; civilian casualties were heavy. But comparatively little damage was done to the factory itself. It happened that Rée had a contact with a member of the Peugeot family, and through him he got in touch with a foreman inside the works who was already organizing a certain amount of that kind of subtle sabotage that makes blame difficult to apportion and therefore avoids the danger of reprisals. A message was sent to London promising to sabotage the factory for as long as the war lasted if the RAF would please keep their bombers away. Agreement was reluctant, but results proved the promise was realistic: production at the factory was permanently disrupted by one means or another, yet the Germans were never able to find out that the damage was being done by teams of workmen inside the works. One day an explosive device intended for the plant's transformers fell from a workman's pocket. A German guard, not recognizing the object, kindly called the man's attention to the fact that he had dropped something.

It is seldom possible to calculate exactly how much one small incident such as the disruption of production at the Peugeot factory contributes to some great event such as the defeat of Germany. And no one can say that a second bomber raid by the RAF might not have been more successful than the first. However, the incident would seem to provide a good example of sabotage proving less costly and–probably–more effective than aerial bombing. A better-known and within its limits indisputable example was the sabotage of the wolfram mines.

Wolfram is the mineral ore from which tungsten is made, and tungsten was a vital war material, being used in both armour plate and in armour-piercing ammunition. There was no satisfactory substitute. The main sources of supply were in the Far East and could not be tapped by Germany. The largest European supplier was Portugal, and although the Germans managed by various means, notably hefty bribery, to acquire some through Spain, operations by the Allies kept the total down. By 1943 German stockpiles (which to the disappointment of the Allies had in fact proved somewhat larger than they had estimated) were running down, and desperate efforts were made to find new sources of supply. One of these was France; there were a number of wolfram mines, mostly in rather remote, mountainous districts, all of them very small, and all idle since the First World War. A number of these mines were reopened by the Germans. As bombing targets they were almost impossible, being small and well-concealed. They did, however, offer a good chance to the saboteur–partly for the same reason. Being small, they could be put out of action by a relatively small amount of damage, being in remote parts they were more vulnerable to guerrilla attack and also required considerable motor-vehicle traffic which, moving along small and deserted roads, offered

Top: The Paris police helped the Free French to clear Paris of Germans.

Opposite top: The French flag being displayed from the windows of a Paris police station in August 1944.

Above: An FFI patrol of local peasants with a captured SS officer near Chartres in August 1944.

Below: A girl accused of collaboration shaved and humiliated by the people of her village.

additional objectives for bomb and booby trap. The chief mine was attacked successfully three times in little over a year; the replacement of civilian miners by soldiers did not prevent a fourth and final capture soon after D-Day. The Resistance was all the more willing to attack the wolfram mines and the vehicles serving them because one of the results of such raids was the capture of supplies of explosive, a commodity as necessary and as scarce as tungsten itself.

The chief object of militant resistance in France, at least as far as Allied command was concerned, was to disrupt communications, notably the railways. In fact railwaymen, not only in France but in other occupied countries also, have a reputation as notably active resisters during the Second World War. The Communists, pointing to their strength in the railway industry, may justifiably take some credit, but there were other causes too, not least the comparative ease of sabotaging a railway system.

Methods of causing difficulties on the railways are too numerous to mention. Introducing an abrasive into lubricants was one favourite tactic (SOE also provided adulterated engine oil for the same purpose), but almost as much trouble could sometimes be caused simply by monkeying with the labels on the trucks or the paperwork in the office, so that a truckload of gunsights expected in Brittany ended up in Provence, while the irritated German gunners found themselves provided with an equivalent quantity of tinned fruit or winter underwear. Overall, it may well be true that what might be called passive sabotage of this type, being so widespread and so difficult to track down to its source, was more effective than sabotage of a more spectacular kind–blowing up engines, tearing up rails, etc.

Immediately before Operation Overlord (the Allied invasion of Normandy in June 1944) Allied command asked the French Resistance for an all-out attack on communications, and the resulting disruption was probably the greatest achievement of the Resistance throughout the war. In some parts of the country the railways were completely out of action for a couple of months before the invasion, and it has been calculated that on the night of 5 June there were almost one thousand individual rail cuts carried out in France. The railways were not the only target. Roads and bridges were also attended to, and great efforts were made to ruin telephone communications.

One result of the desperate state of transport and communications, accompanied by harassment from irregulars, was that German reinforcements took a long time to reach the battle area. The *Reich* division took three weeks to get from the Garonne to Normandy, and the fury and frustration this bred in one SS unit belonging to it resulted in the massacre of Oradour, where some 600 women and children were burned to death in the village church–probably the worst of all the German atrocities in France.

But the disruption of the transport and communication system in the spring and summer of 1944 was not, of course, solely the work of the French Resistance. For weeks before Overlord Allied aeroplanes had pounded railway yards, bridges and important junctions throughout France. It would be hard to judge the relative effect of the Allied bombs and Resistance sabotage in hampering German movements. Eisenhower's remark that the Resistance was worth fifteen divisions may have been partly good politics; Montgomery, to name only one other Allied general, rated the contribution of the Resistance much lower.

Although not much direct assistance could be offered in Normandy, which was naturally thick with troops and armour, in Brittany and other parts of France the Maquis emerged from cover to harass the Germans. The activities of the Resistance generally rose to a very high pitch, and counter-resistance mounted correspondingly, with many acts of particular savagery provoked on the one hand by hatred long-suppressed and on the other by frustration and fear of defeat. 'Collaborators' were pursued with ferocity and, in parts of the country, there was something like civil war.

In Paris itself, oddly enough, the news of the Normandy landings caused very little apparent excitement. Rumour had been so frequent and so false a visitor during the previous four years that many were slow to believe the news was true. Even when Wehrmacht signs began to appear in Paris streets marked 'To the Normandy Front', there was no great excitement. But the mood began to change on that famous anniversary, 14 July; Parisians suddenly realised that liberation was at hand. Anti-German acts increased. The *Front National* put up inflammatory posters inciting assassination of enemies, the chief object being the *Milice* rather than the Germans. Ordinary life, insofar as life in occupied Paris was ever ordinary, began to break down. The electricity supply, already subject to regular shut-downs, tended to fail more frequently, and other services grew increasingly unreliable, while theatres and other forms of entertainment closed their doors. As it became clear that the Allies would shortly capture the city, there were signs of cracking discipline among the German garrison; a number of men deserted. De Gaulle, back in Algiers after a quick trip to North America, saw the moment of crisis at hand. Paris, as he wrote in his memoirs, had become 'the centre point of strategy and the heart of politics'. Berlin appointed a new commander, Dietrich von Choltitz, to organize the evacuation of the French capital.

The Americans were coming, everyone – friend and enemy – was thinking. But when? In fact, Paris had ceased to be an important strategic target, whatever de Gaulle or other Frenchmen might think, and General Omar Bradley was planning to bypass the city, leaving the German garrison safely bottled up in the rear of his advance, to surrender in their own good time. The Parisians themselves forced a change of plan.

It is hard to pin down the precise origins of the Paris Rising. On 10 August there was a railway strike; five days later, when the Germans began to disarm the police, they went on strike. This was decisive, for the police, who had on the whole a good reputation with the Resistance, had hitherto kept civil order. On 15 August nearly all the life-support systems of Paris came to a stop. Germans were leaving by whatever means they could. On 17 August the *tricolore* began to appear on certain buildings.

Most responsible people were opposed to a violent rising, preferring to wait until the Allied forces arrived. But Communist leaders in the Resistance insisted on instant revolt, and others, particularly de Gaulle's representatives and supporters, recognized that they could not afford to sit quietly while the Communists led the people of Paris against their oppressors. There were also psychological reasons in favour of a popular rising, but it cannot be said that it made any sense from a military angle.

The Rising can be said to have begun on 19 August when 2,000 policemen stood at attention in the court of the Prefecture singing the *Marseillaise*. Some of the earliest casualties were suffered when the Germans attempted to recapture the Prefecture later that day. Of those who died during the next five days, a significant proportion were innocent passers-by killed by accident, members of the FFI shot mistakenly by their comrades, collaborators or alleged collaborators assassinated by members, sometimes self-proclaimed members, of the Resistance. Much of the actual street fighting was done by teenage boys.

Almost as soon as the rising began the Swedish consul, Raoul Nordling, attempted to arrange a truce to save the city from destruction. The truce never really took hold, but it created a couple of days of comparative lull which gave the Resistance a chance to organize and to publish papers on how to make a Molotov cocktail or build a street barricade.

Building barricades is, of course, something that comes naturally to the citizens of Paris, like breaching the dikes to the Dutch. The chunky stones with which the Paris streets are paved might almost have been designed to be used to build defence works, and some of the barricades thrown up in August 1944 were remarkably well-constructed fortifications of which Vauban himself might have approved. They were manned 24 hours a day by relays of young men with rifles and home-made bombs, supplied with food and telephone communications by nearby shops, and linked by a messenger system of boys and girls on bicycles. Although there were heavy casualties at some of the barricades, on the whole the Germans were not particularly aggressive. They had no more than 100 tanks, and little or no high explosive was used, only machine guns and armour-piercing shells. The fighting included some comic or absurd incidents—large detachments of well-armed Germans surrendering to one man with an armband; a group of German officers demanding of their solitary American prisoner that he should take *them* under *his* protection—and it also had moments of grim horror and tragic irony. Damage to buildings was slight, but the Grand Palais was set on fire by German incendiaries. Some circus animals in the park escaped, were killed, accidentally or not, by gunfire, and hastily dismembered by the meat-starved citizens.

The outbreak of the revolt in Paris forced a change in Allied plans. It was clearly desirable to effect the capture of the capital as quickly as possible, and Bradley despatched General Leclerc's French 2nd Armoured Division towards Paris.

Choltitz had orders to raze Paris, but they were never carried out. It is unlikely that he could have committed such an outrage even if he had wished to do so, as the German garrison, which was not very strong and was confined to a small part of the city, simply did not have the explosives to do the job. But fighting within the city was getting fiercer. On 23 August the British Broadcasting Corporation announced somewhat prematurely that Paris was free, and the fiercest fighting so far was witnessed, but at about 17.00 hours a small aeroplane flew in low over the Prefecture of Police and dropped a message from Leclerc: *'Tenez bon. Nous arrivons!'* ('Hold on. We're coming!').

In fact Leclerc had made rather slow progress, having encountered somewhat stiffer German resistance than expected outside Paris. Bradley suspected that the delay was due to the welcoming celebrations at towns and villages along the way, and remarking testily that he was not going to wait until the French 'danced their way to Paris', ordered in an American division also. Possibly the move hastened Leclerc's entry, for as Choltitz was gloomily sipping his last post-prandial brandy in the diminishing German enclave in Paris, he heard the bells of Nôtre Dame signalling the arrival at the gates of the city of the first of Leclerc's tanks.

The next day, 25 August, was the day of liberation; yet a few German strongholds remained. Most of them were willing to surrender to regular troops, and the FFI took at least one strongpoint unaided by Leclerc's men; but there was hard and unrelenting combat at some points where groups of SS men defied their officers and refused to contemplate surrender. At 16.00 hours de Gaulle arrived. His first visit was to Leclerc's headquarters in the Gare Montparnasse rather than the Resistance leaders' headquarters in the Hotel de Ville. From Leclerc de Gaulle went to his old office in the war department where, he says, 'Not a piece of furniture, not a rug, not a curtain had been disturbed. On the desk, the telephone was in the same place, and exactly the same names were on the call buttons.' Only then did he go to meet the leaders of the Resistance.

For a day or two after the surrender of the German garrison, indiscriminate shooting could be heard in Paris. When de Gaulle entered Nôtre Dame there were even shots fired from the clerestory. At least some of the shooting could probably be put down, as de Gaulle asserted, to left-wing elements attempting to keep a revolution going. Meanwhile a ghastly settling of old scores was going on.

Yet in Paris, among the broken glass, people danced in the warm summer evening. Old friends reappeared, old relationships were re-established or perhaps severed, old mysteries explained. In the street children scrambled happily over derelict German tanks.

Above: A group of hostages being executed by the Italians at Celje, in Slovenia, in July 1942.

Below: Četnik soldiers in action in the mountains; the terrain was of great assistance to the guerrillas.

Yugoslavia

THE COUNTRY now known as Yugoslavia emerged from the wreckage of the old eastern European empires after the First World War. It was originally known as the Kingdom of the Serbs, Croats and Slovenes, but in fact it was a far greater national hotch-potch than even that clumsy title suggested. It contained a large number of minority groups all of whom were more or less dissatisfied with their lot; this made Yugoslavia's relations with its immediate neighbours difficult. The chief domestic conflict, however, was between the dominant Serbs and the Croats, and it was largely that conflict which ensured the failure of democracy–such as it was– in Yugoslavia between the wars. As the system was on the point of complete breakdown, the king, Alexander, stepped in, assuming responsibility for government and becoming virtually a dictator. Alexander was Serb to the backbone, and though he did make some efforts to reconcile the Croats, his success was limited, while his denial of democracy alienated others. Whatever further moves Alexander may have contemplated, all came to nought in 1934 when he was assassinated, with the French foreign minister, in Marseille. The assassination was the work of the Ustaše, an extremist Croatian group linked to the Fascists in Italy.

As Alexander's son was a boy of fourteen, his uncle, Prince Paul, became regent (actually he was one of three co-regents, but the others counted for little). The problems remained, and Paul was no more capable of solving them than Alexander had been; but quite soon Yugoslavia's domestic problems began to seem less important because of greater dangers looming abroad. Though linked with France and Britain, Yugoslavia's main economic partner was Germany, which took the major part of her exported raw materials, including certain minerals. During the 1930s, the economy of the country became tied ever more closely to Germany, and the regent Paul saw no alternative to a pro-German policy except total collapse. The crisis over Czechoslovakia in 1938 was seen by the Yugoslavs more realistically than it was in Britain, where Neville Chamberlain apparently believed that ceding the Sudetenland to Hitler would prevent further German aggression against the Czechs. The Yugoslavs were not deceived; but the lesson drawn from Munich by the Yugoslav government was that as no help could be expected from the West, a policy agreeable to Hitler was all the more vital. Between 1939 and 1941 Yugoslavia became virtually a German satellite, and in March 1941 the government reluctantly agreed to sign the Tripartite Pact which, among other things, conceded to Germany the right to move troops across Yugoslav territory. The signing of the pact was fiercely resented at many levels of Yugoslav society, and it provoked a *coup d'etat*. Prince Paul was deposed, the young King Peter declared of age (a little prematurely as he was not yet eighteen) and a new government formed under General Dušan Simović. In essence the change meant little, and in any case the government lasted only a few days. A furious Hitler ordered the immediate invasion of Yugoslavia. As Churchill remarked, the Yugoslavs had saved their souls but at the cost of their territory.

Yugoslavia was already virtually surrounded, most of its neighbours– Austria, Hungary, Rumania, Bulgaria, Albania (not yet Greece)–being already under Axis control. That made things easier for the Germans. Moreover, the Yugoslav armed forces were small and–by German standards–primitive, in spite of the splendid military tradition of Serbia. Mobilization was so slow that many men had not reached their units when the ten days of fighting ended on 17 April with the formal surrender of the Yugoslav forces and the disintegration of Yugoslavia.

The country was split up into numerous parts. Slovenia was divided between Germany and Italy, which also controlled most of the Adriatic coast and islands as well as Montenegro (nominally an independent state), while some southern districts became part of Albania, which was also under Italian control. Bulgaria and Hungary received neighbouring chunks of what had been Yugoslavia, though Rumania declined her slice of cake, and the Germans had to take it over. That left Croatia and Serbia, each–especially Serbia–considerably truncated. For practical purposes, Croatia came under the government of the Ustaše and their leader, Ante Pavelić, who instituted a reign of terror, directed mainly against Serbs and Jews, quite as horrifying as the Nazis perpetrated anywhere else in Europe. Serbia, or what remained of it, was governed by a native administration under General Milan Nedić, who was in effect a German puppet with virtually no free will.

Although the German government had on file plans for invading the Balkans, the invasion had actually been provoked by the coup in Belgrade, and was not part of Hitler's immediate strategy. Except for the communications route to the south via Belgrade and the Morava River, Yugoslavia was of little strategic significance so far as Hitler was concerned. In the spring of 1941 the project chiefly on his mind was the invasion of Russia, which had to be postponed partly because of the diversion of troops against Yugoslavia. It followed that once the country had been conquered, many of the invading troops, including all the best fighting units, were withdrawn in preparation for the drive to the east. It was this absence of front-line troops which largely accounted for the remarkable successes of anti-Axis guerrillas later in the year.

Some of the earliest resistance groups were formed of men who had been on their way to join their units when the surrender came. Although the Germans rounded up 300,000 Serbian officers and men, soldiers of other nationalities were mostly released. There was, inevitably, much confusion, with thousands of men wandering about, some making their way into the plentiful mountains, others picking up the vast quantities of weapons left lying around in the general muddle. The situation inside the country long remained in this state of confusion.

Everyone knows that the irregular war against the Germans and Italians and their allies in occupied Yugoslavia was also a civil war and that there were two rival guerrilla armies, Communist and non-Communist. There were, however, an enormous number of different groups involved, and Yugoslavs were divided not only by politics but by race, religion, class and almost every other conceivable human diversity. Yet these divisions were often blurred, and those who were locked in murderous hostility in one region might be found apparently co-operating amiably in another. The situation is not made clearer by the fact that the history of these years is still often written too much in black and white when, as one British official in the Balkans said during the war, the predominant shade in Yugoslavia (as elsewhere) is grey.

The savagery of the conflicts between Serb and Croat, Christian and Moslem, Communist and monarchist, as well as occupier and occupied, was often horrifying, and generated greater violence, more determined resistance. In Bosnia, Serbian villagers were accustomed to move with their flocks higher up the mountains during the summer months. Faced with persecution, they did the same thing, leaving their villages deserted when the Ustaše gangs arrived. Others, of course, were unable to escape in such ways. It has been estimated that 600,000 people were killed by fellow-Slavs between 1941 and 1945 (perhaps half that number being Serbs accounted for by the genocidal Ustaše). One atrocity provoked another, and in regions where the population was mixed each community tried to drive the others from its territory. One of the greatest strengths of the Communists was that they were above this fratricidal strife, not only in theory but in action too. Though they were not immune to vengeance and the violence it provoked, they generally treated the civilian population of towns they occupied better than their opponents.

After the debacle of the German invasion in April 1941, a number of officers and men of the defeated army took shelter in the mountains of western Serbia under the leadership of Colonel Draža Mihailović. They became known as Četniks. In some ways this was a rather unfortunate name. Literally, it means members of a *četa*, or armed company, but in the past it had been used particularly of Serbian irregulars fighting against the Turks. Not only was it an exclusively Serbian term, thus reinforcing

the essentially Serbian character of Mihailović's organization, but it was also used by several other groups not operating under Mihailović's control. In 1941 there was already an official body known as Četniks, who subsequently served the Nedić government in Serbia. Thus, when there was talk of Četniks co-operating with Italians or Germans, it was not always Mihailović's Četniks who were responsible. Not only Yugoslav civilians suffered confusion on this point. .

In different circumstances, Mihailović might have been a Yugoslavian de Gaulle. As a regular soldier before the war (and for a short time director of military intelligence), he had the reputation of being a bit of a lone wolf, less respectful towards his superiors than they would have liked, and too clever for his own good. It was typical of him that in April 1941 he simply refused to accept the order to capitulate and at once made his way to the mountain plateau of Ravna Gora where he set up his headquarters and began to build up his underground organization. But, a gloomy-looking man of slightish build, Mihailović lacked charisma. His main purpose was not, anyway, to carry on the war against the Germans. He was an intensely patriotic Serb with little interest in the other Yugoslav peoples, loyal to the Serbian monarchy, fiercely anti-Communist. Like some other European resistance leaders belonging to the military establishment, he was more concerned with what would happen when the war ended than with making a contribution towards ending it. He believed that the war would last a long time, and in the meantime his role was to be the guardian of the pre-war state and the pre-war system. He was on the whole opposed to active resistance because he did not believe it could do much good – and certainly it did great harm in the shape of reprisals against the civilian population. To some extent, Mihailović was overtaken by events, for resistance to the Germans did break out in Serbia soon after the defeat, and on a larger scale than might have been expected. Mihailović himself was in a way responsible, for his success in building up an underground army encouraged resistance. Nevertheless, Mihailović was not in favour of a serious rising against the Germans unless it was combined with an Allied invasion of the Balkans – an event that he, like most others, believed was probable – leading swiftly to total liberation. Until it came, he was concerned to strengthen his organization and defeat his rivals, especially the Communists, not to waste his resources in what he regarded as futile resistance.

The German invasion of Russia was seen to be a step that would lead inevitably to Hitler's defeat. In Serbia particularly, the popular mood changed from despair to optimism. Resistance by all groups was greatly encouraged. The attack on Russia also brought the Communists into the battle (they had been preparing for it for some time, and had about five weeks' notice of Operation Barbarossa).

Although not numerous, the Yugoslav Communist Party was well equipped for resistance. It had been illegal since 1921 and was therefore already accustomed to an underground existence. Its leading members were not only trained in the techniques of secret political opposition, many of them were also veterans of the Spanish Civil War. Moreover, since the party had been banned during the 1920s and 1930s, it had taken no part in the petty, sometimes vicious, political conflicts of that time, and attracted to its ranks many of the best young people who were understandably disillusioned with democratic politics though in many cases not Communists themselves. Finally, the Communist Party had the advantage of outstanding leadership. Its general secretary, later war leader and statesman, was one of the greatest men of his time. Josip Brož, better known by his code name Tito, came from a poor Catholic family in Croatia. He fought in the Great War as an Austrian conscript and was captured by the Russians. He was a prisoner in Russia during the Revolution, and during the 1930s he worked for the Comintern in various countries. At length he was given the job of reconstructing the Yugoslav Communist Party, which was on the point of total collapse. He very rapidly strengthened, expanded and unified it. When the Germans invaded the Soviet Union, of which Tito remained at that time a faithful servant, he gave the order for a rising: 'You cannot stand idly by while the precious blood of the heroic people of Soviet Russia is shed', ran the Central

Committee's hastily roneoed proclamation. Tito's aims were of course directly opposed to those of Mihailović. He did not want to preserve the status quo; on the contrary, he wanted revolution, and the war, as the First World War had done in Russia, would help to bring the Revolution about. His strategy was almost the direct opposite of Mihailović's; he wanted an all-out popular revolt, a national liberation movement, which would be led, naturally, by the Communist Party. He was not to be intimidated by reprisals (though later he took care to guard against reprisals, since they led to resentment of those who provoked them as well as those who carried them out).

Given this almost total contradiction of aims, it is hardly surprising that the Partisans (i.e. Tito's Communists) and the Četniks (i.e. Mihailović's Serbian monarchists) failed to agree (even their hair styles were different, the Partisans being cropped short while the Četniks grew long hair and beards, in the tradition of bereaved males in the Orthodox Church). To begin with, there was some co-operation. Many Četniks were just as anxious as the Partisans to have a crack at the enemy, and the two groups combined in a number of attacks on towns and communications in western Serbia. But there were differences and eventually clashes. Genuine efforts were made by both sides to come to an agreement, but as time passed the chances, always slight, of co-operation disappeared altogether.

The various resistance forces in Yugoslavia had remarkable success during the summer of 1941. By September they held most of western Serbia outside the larger towns, though this was made possible by the weakness of the occupying forces rather than the strength of the resistance. On 24 September the Partisans captured the town of Užice which, among other advantages, had a bank full of money and an arms factory making rifles. Under Partisan administration, the output of rifles was greatly increased. (Užice also had a printing press, on which a history of the Yugoslav Communist Party was printed – a sign that the future was not forgotten.) These successes tended to exacerbate the conflict between Partisans and Četniks because of jealousy over booty; the Partisans did promise to give some rifles to the Četniks, who, however, infuriated the Partisans by handing over a large group of prisoners to the Germans and attacking Partisan-held Užice, though unsuccessfully.

Partisan successes provoked reprisals. The most notorious took place in October in the town of Kragujevac, where a few days before the Germans had suffered a dozen or so casualties in a brush with Partisans. The entire male population over the age of 15, about 5,000 men and boys, was shot in batches of 100 at a time in the course of one day. This shatteringly evil deed (some members of the German firing squads themselves suffered nervous collapse) had the predictable result of confirming Mihailović in his determination not to fight the Germans and confirming Tito in his determination to fight as hard as possible.

There was little chance to attack at this time, however, for the Germans launched the first of a series of offensives against the Partisans, drove them out of their conquests, including Užice, and forced them to withdraw altogether from Serbia through the mountains into Bosnia, with their pursuers a rifle shot away. They took their wounded with them, as they were to do throughout the war, sometimes in seemingly impossible circumstances; they would not leave them for the Germans. At Palisad, the Germans had finished off wounded Partisans by driving tanks over them.

While the Partisans retreated into remote mountain regions where they might be safe though not comfortable, the Četniks were left comparatively undisturbed at Ravna Gora. Mihailović had turned down Tito's request for aid in slowing down the Germans when they were hot on the Partisans' trail, and some Četnik leaders were undoubtedly in cahoots with the Germans (though not Mihailović himself). By the end of the year, the rising in Serbia had been thoroughly suppressed and no more 'liberated areas' remained in the hands of the Partisans. At about the same time the Italians finally succeeded in quieting Montenegro, where a general revolt, led partly by Communists taking advantage of that partiality for the Russians which was as strong in Montenegro as in Serbia, had considerable success for a time against the relatively amiable occupation of the Italians. Later, fighting broke out in Montenegro between rival national and religious groups – Communists (who had lost some popularity through harsh policies of a type they avoided in other regions) against Četniks, Orthodox against Muslim, etc. The Italians merely stood aside and, as in Croatia, allowed the various groups to fight each other.

The year 1942 was a decisive one for Yugoslavia. The Balkans generally were coming to figure more prominently in German strategy. The supply line for Rommel's forces in North Africa ran through Belgrade, and the Germans aimed to keep Partisans at a safe distance from it.

In January Mihailović was appointed minister of war in the Yugoslav government in exile (the King and his ministers had escaped to London in 1941). He was still determined to avoid unnecessary blood-letting, and would not consider a full-scale rising unless it was certain to lead to the swift liberation of the country. He kept only a small staff with him permanently, and the remainder went, or were sent, home. Many of them enlisted in the state guard of Nedić's Serb puppet government. This had certain advantages, as long as the men concerned could be trusted to remain loyal to Mihailović, and certainly provided Četnik headquarters with good intelligence as well as some weapons, but it had obvious disadvantages also, not the least being that it inevitably cast further doubt on Mihailović's true aims. To the Partisans, of course, it was already clear that Mihailović was much more interested in suppressing native Communists than foreign invaders. Nevertheless, a good deal of sabotage was carried out by the Četniks during 1942, especially after Allied requests for action in the autumn.

In the spring Mihailović himself left his base in Serbia and moved into northern Montenegro. He was known throughout Yugoslavia and found that he was offered leadership of groups calling themselves Četniks in Montenegro, Bosnia and other parts. These groups varied a great deal in composition and intention, and many of them were almost totally negative–against the old Yugoslavia which Mihailović represented as much as the new Yugoslavia which Tito was coming to represent. They were willing to acknowledge Mihailović as their commander merely in order to give themselves some kind of apparent legitimacy in their own districts, and also because through him they could get weapons–or at least hoped to get them. They were not really interested in what Mihailović stood for, still less in listening to and obeying his orders. Mihailović himself lacked the personality to impose his authority on these wayward resisters, and the plain fact was that, outside Serbia, he had very little influence.

In January 1942 Tito set up his headquarters in the little town of Foča, where he remained for nearly six months. Those who had come over the mountains with him formed the core of the first 'Proletarian Brigade'. There was no attempt to disguise the fact of Communist leadership of the Partisans, and although non-Communists were formed into 'volunteer' units, they too had their political commissar attached to look after the education of the volunteers. The name 'proletarian brigade' in fact earned Tito a rebuke from what at first seems an unlikely source–the Soviet Union. At this time the Russians were in favour of a combined resistance in Yugoslavia and were afraid that Tito would upset the Allies. To Tito's anger, the Soviet Union even gave the Četniks credit for actions performed by the Partisans. Such propaganda was to be expected from the British, but Tito objected angrily to Moscow following the same line, and even secured an apology of a sort.

Although Tito made no secret of the Communist organization of the Partisans, he was careful to avoid any suggestion of a 'class war' in his movement, something his opponents were eager to attach to him. The Partisans' avoidance of national, religious and class hatreds drew to them many new recruits, including Croats (originally, the Partisans were largely Serb, although Tito himself was a Croat).

Tito was anxious to turn the Partisans into a regular military force; he followed guerrilla tactics because he had to, not because he preferred them. Discipline was strict, and punishments for insubordination severe. Each brigade (of about 1,000 men each) had its own headquarters, its own transport, artillery and medical units, however sparsely equipped these might be. Men marched under the Partisan flag–a five-pointed star on a red ground with hammer and sickle in one corner. Young women were also recruited and took part in action. They suffered heavy casualties: 'They are not accustomed to fighting', wrote Vladimir Dedijer in his diary (*With Tito Through the War*, London 1951), 'and do not know how to take cover.'

Discipline was necessary in order to preserve the best possible relations

Top left: Draža Mihailović found that his Serbian nationalism limited the appeal of the Četniks in the rest of Yugoslavia.

Top right: Tito, photographed here in 1943, was perhaps the greatest leader to emerge from the partisan fighting of the Second World War.

Above: Popular demonstrations at the downfall of the government of Prince Paul in March 1941.

Above: Tito and Churchill at their meeting at Caserta, near Naples, in September 1944.

Below: The Partisans on the march with their wounded in hay-filled carts in the summer of 1944.

Above: Women Partisans training at an Allied camp in Italy, veterans of guerrilla warfare in Yugoslavia.

Below: A detachment of Partisans, now in control of most of Yugoslavia, advancing through Bosnia in 1945.

with the civilian population. Tito and his comrades were well aware of the much-quoted proverb of the Chinese partisans (now usually attributed to Mao) to the effect that partisans in a community are like fish living in a river; the river can exist without the fish, but not the fish without the river. 'It is essential,' ran a Partisan directive quoted by Phyllis Auty (*Tito*, London 1970), 'to build up close relations between army and civilians so that the people feels itself one with the military . . . The correct functioning of even the smallest organs of government is the very basis for success in the war of liberation; without this the greatest victories in the field are built on sand.' Food was not plundered, and when taken was paid for. When some Partisan horses got into a peasant woman's wheatfield and did considerable damage to the crop, she was given half a hundredweight of maize as compensation while the men in charge of the horses were placed under arrest. The area in which the Partisans operated throughout the war was never at the best of times self-sufficient in food. Yet in spite of almost constant hunger, few actually starved. Much food was smuggled in from the rich valley of the Sava, often at great risk – a sign of the support the Partisans derived from the peasants.

During the early months of 1942 the Second and Third Offensives were launched against the Partisans and other groups by the Germans acting in co-operation with the Ustaše, though the latter were already showing signs of disintegration. At the end of May, Tito left Foča but, instead of returning towards Serbia as his men had expected, he wisely decided to move farther west in search of greater security. The 'Great March', as the Partisans came to call it, took them into the area of western Bosnia and southern Croatia. It lasted over three months. About 3,000 people took part and there were many wounded, which slowed progress, but the march ended in success and brighter prospects for the victory of the Partisans.

The Partisans had since the beginning learned to live hard, and hard living was all they had for a very long time. With the exception of rare feasts, they were constantly short of food, or of food of the right kind. Many a dinner was made of nettles, while fighting units sometimes existed for days on an exclusive diet of herbs. To a newly arrived British liaison officer in 1943 Vladimir Dedijer recommended young beech leaves as the basis of a salad with sorrel and wild garlic. Basil Davidson, who served with the Partisans in Hungarian-occupied Yugoslavia, used to shoot the occasional slow-lolloping hare, and F. W. D. Deakin wrote of 'quenching our thirst from the dew on the fir cones, and broiling clover and wild spinach in our mess tins' (*The Embattled Mountain*, London 1971). Precious dynamite was used occasionally to stun trout in a river, but that was rare. Months of poor diet had its inevitable effect on health. There were even cases of scurvy, and doctors found that wounds took three times longer to heal.

Hunger was perhaps the most pervasive impression of the Great March. Hunger and damp. There seemed to be far more rain than normal that year, and clothes were often damp for days on end. Crouching under a roof of branches, with an eye out for Italian aeroplanes, listening to the radio or playing chess, tired, dirty and hungry men remained in remarkably high spirits, held together by the comradeship of shared beliefs and shared experience, singing old ballads or new Partisan songs. Deeds of horror or heroism were numerous: many examples can be found in the accounts of British liaison officers who served with the Partisans, or in the diary of Dedijer. He recorded, for example, an unnamed girl of the Zlatarski battalion who was wounded in an engagement with Četniks. Having fired her last shot she jumped over a cliff to avoid being captured alive. However, she was caught on some rocks half way down and later rescued by the Partisans.

Sometimes they passed into a quiet valley, where the river flowed, the trees blossomed and bore fruit, and all was green and silent: no sign of human life. It was, said Tito, as if a magician had waved his wand over the place and banished humanity from it. At this place Tito discovered on a patch of rising ground strawberries, '... unbelievable wealth,' as Dedijer said. 'In half an hour I had gathered a plate full, and eaten them all ...'

Desire for a comfortable resting place and for good food often occupied the mind. 'Our main topic is beautiful food,' wrote a British sergeant with the Partisans a year later. 'I dreamed of boiled apple pudding and custard.' Rain falling through the beech trees, the air so damp that paper would hardly burn and old wounds ached anew, lice biting at the scalp, the temptation to think that the next man had a larger helping of gruel—a teaspoon more at least—these were the facts of Partisan existence. At other times bombs fell, mortars pounded, or machine guns chattered of death. Perhaps worst of all was the evidence of human evil. After describing the atrocities committed in one village by the Ustaše, Milovan Djilas wrote, 'life is not worth living in this world while there are men who commit such inhumanities'.

The Partisans also had some welcome strokes of luck. They reached a village called Bradina just as a goods train was pulling out. They raced towards the station and captured the train, as well as half a ton of dynamite which they used to carry out some very effective sabotage of the railway line. But the captured train itself was an unexpected delight; fruit, honey, cloth, motor cycles were on board, and more fruit, liqueurs and two sackfulls of biscuits were found in the station buffet. It was like Christmas.

In the autumn of 1942 the Partisans gained control of a large area in western Bosnia, extending into Croatia, the total equalling the area of Switzerland. Less than a year after they had seemed to be on the point of total collapse, they were flourishing as never before, their numbers up and rising daily. Early in November they captured the town of Bihać from the Ustaše, and this became virtually the capital of a Partisan state. Tito did not actually set up a government in name, having been urged not to do so by the Soviet Union, which did not want unnecessary trouble with London as a result of such an obvious challenge to the Yugoslav government in exile. The body that was set up was called the National Liberation Executive Committee, and it contained non-Communist representatives, including members of the pre-war political parties. Nevertheless, leadership remained firmly in Communist hands.

At the end of 1942 Yugoslavia had not yet become very important in the eyes of the opponents to Hitler, who were too preoccupied with defending themselves. Nevertheless, the great powers were not unaware of what was happening in Yugoslavia. Radio transmissions from Mihailović had been picked up three or four months after the German invasion, and the first British liaison officer, Captain 'Bill' Hudson, had been landed on the coast in October 1941. Hudson spent time with the Partisans as well as the Četniks, and though he was out of touch with his superiors for a long period due to the loss of his transmitter, the British also knew of the Partisans at a comparatively early date. Since they were only interested in opposition to the Germans, not with internal Yugoslav affairs, the British were anxious to bring Partisans and Četniks together; all British liaison officers were charged with this attempt, in which the Soviet Union also co-operated. However, since Mihailović was the representative of the Yugoslav government in exile (indeed, a minister in it), which was recognized by the British–and the Soviet Union–as the rightful government of the country, it was to Mihailović that aid was sent. Yet before the end of 1942, and perhaps much earlier, the British were aware, first, that Mihailović's chief preoccupation was not fighting the Germans and the Italians but preventing the Communists from carrying through a revolution in Yugoslavia and, second, that the Partisans were causing the Axis forces considerable difficulty. Indeed, this had been known possibly since late 1941. There is a note in the files of the Foreign Office dated July 1942 which runs 'as we know ... any activity in Yugoslavia should really be attributed to the Partisans, but, for public consumption, we can see no harm in a certain amount of this going to the credit of Mihailović'. (quoted by Elizabeth Barker, 'Some Factors in British Decision-making over Yugoslavia 1941-4' in Phyllis Auty and Richard Clogg (eds.) *British Policy Towards Wartime Resistance in Yugoslavia ...*, London 1975).

Not surprisingly, Tito was extremely bitter that the Četniks, who were fighting him rather than the Germans or Italians, were receiving aid from Britain while he, who really was fighting the Axis, was not. He remained suspicious of the British for a long time, and the mystery of the Atherton mission–a British party murdered in April 1942 whose deaths were falsely ascribed to Tito–did not help.

However, the actual aid that Britain was sending at this time to Mihailović was rather small. The aircraft were not available, nor were the supplies. Various British officials sometimes became very angry with Mihailović for not pursuing a more active policy without appreciating that, since the aid Mihailović was receiving from Britain was so paltry, he had small motive for acting as the British wanted. And not only was

British aid on a small scale; it was often hopelessly inappropriate and no aid whatever. Colonel S. W. Bailey, who was British liaison officer with Mihailović, reports that in the ten weeks after his arrival, an event which Mihailović naturally took to presage greater British supplies, only two sorties were made, and of the few tons dropped, a proportion consisted of a large quantity of Italian occupation paper money overprinted ETHIOPIA in bright red and 'several hundred boxes of tropical anti-snake-bite serum'. (A year later, when the Partisans were beginning to get British supplies from North Africa, a request for anti-aircraft guns produced two barrels of what the British liaison officer had to explain, with considerable embarrassment, were fly-swatters. The Partisans said that they did not think they could knock out German aircraft with those.)

Tito might have expected better from his masters in the Soviet Union, to whom he sent regular reports and frequent compelling pleas for medical supplies, weapons, boots and uniforms and, above all, ammunition. In spite of the difficulties that the Russians themselves were in, there seemed to be every likelihood of such supplies being sent. A message from Moscow in February 1942 mentioned the possibility of sending men and requested details for landing aircraft in Partisan territory. But soon afterwards the Soviet tone changed somewhat. A host of difficulties seemed to have arisen. The men waiting in the cold for the Soviet aircraft to arrive on a bleak and windy plateau in Montenegro waited in vain. 'All possible efforts are being made to help you with armaments,' Tito's Soviet contact assured him, 'but technical difficulties are enormous.' It seems evident that the Soviet government had decided to withhold help from Tito in order not to antagonize the West. Thus the Partisans fought alone through the most difficult period, when they were struggling to survive. They received no help from the British until the middle of 1943, and none from the Soviet Union until 1944.

The experiences of 1941 had shown that the Partisans could not face the occupying forces in open country, and they had therefore withdrawn to the central mountainous area of Bosnia-Hercegovina and Montenegro, regions which were not of interest in themselves to the Italians or the Germans. But the presence of the Partisans in a position to threaten communications or to co-ordinate a rising with an Allied invasion of the Adriatic coast was a constant worry even when actual sabotage was limited in extent. And during 1943 the activities of the Partisans increased.

In 1943 the Allies were becoming increasingly interested in what was happening in Eastern Europe. The invasion of Italy took place in the summer and Allied propaganda had encouraged the myth of a Balkan landing in every way possible in order to tie down enemy troops. It was also decided that, since the attempt to get resistance groups in Yugoslavia to co-operate with each other had clearly failed, they should make contact with Tito's Partisans.

Meanwhile the Germans became increasingly anxious about their communications from Greece to Italy and the various minerals, comparatively small in quantity, which they drew from Yugoslavia. They therefore decided on a renewal of the attempt to detroy the Yugoslav guerrilla forces. Early in 1943 they began the Fourth Offensive (called by the Germans Operation White) which was followed after a brief lull in the spring by the Fifth Offensive (Operation Black). The German plan was first to encircle the Partisan-liberated area in Bosnia and annihilate the Partisan army. Secondly, they would turn against the Četniks, who would have assisted in operations against the Partisans, and disarm them.

The plan failed when the pincers failed to close, largely due to poor coordination of the German with the increasingly dilatory Italian forces, and Tito was again able to break out to the south. Djilas had been in Split where he had learned in advance of the German plans, but all the same it was a close-run thing and the main Partisan army in Bosnia, 25,000 strong, narrowly escaped annihilation at the Neretva River.

The retreat was no rout, but a fighting withdrawal, with the Partisan 'shock brigades' launching diversionary attacks on enemy targets. As usual, the Partisans took their wounded with them, but the task was a daunting one. By the end of February their wounded numbered about 4,000, not counting typhus victims, and during the retreat the total grew daily. At times they were subjected to bombing by Dorniers and Stukas, against which they had no real defence. At the Neretva River, Dedijer recorded impressions in his diary:

'The enemy has us surrounded–Germans advancing from Vakuf, Germans and Četniks from Konjic, Germans and legionaries from Ravno, Italians and Četniks from Duvno. We are hemmed in the Rama valley, with the canyon of the Neretva before us and the swift river–250 feet wide–on the far side the cliffs of Mt Prenj, rising to over 7,000 feet! And Četniks around on every peak. Then the sky from dawn to dusk, full of aircraft...

[The bridge] is nothing but a basketwork affair. Weaving through the confusion of the destroyed railway bridge, among the overturned trucks, is a bridge of narrow planking. 25,000 soldiers and wounded men have to cross by it. But the approach is terrible. Even a man in the pink of health would feel dizzy, let alone a wounded man. The track is wet and full of holes. Wounded men are crawling down on it, on all fours, all shouting, carrying stretcher cases–horses falling with their pack ... below, the Nerevta, foaming–on the hills all around, mortars firing, altogether a terrible picture...'

(*With Tito Through the War*, Alexander Hamilton, London 1951, pages 284 and 287-8)

Tito called on Moscow for help, only to get the usual reply about insuperable technical difficulties and a promise that, of course, all would be done just as soon as the difficulties were overcome. However, the Partisans saved themselves by their own efforts. The Četniks were defeated, and the main Partisan army escaped into Montenegro (by this time Tito commanded forces in many parts of Yugoslavia). The mountains, which were the *sine qua non* of partisans warfare, could on occasions work against the Partisans. Tito remarked that during this offensive, the mountainous terrain was nearly disastrous in slowing the retreating Partisans down at a time when clear weather opened up the skies for German bombers.

Things were becoming even more complicated in Yugoslavia in 1943. As F. B. Singleton put it, 'The ramifications of treachery, collaborationism, opportunism and sheer incoherence, the tangled web of motives, the tortuous labyrinths of plot and counter-plot have an air of Gilbertian absurdity – until one realises that the future of a heroic people was at stake.' (Muriel Heppell and F. B. Singleton, *Yugoslavia*, Benn, 1961.)

Even Tito entered into discussion with the Germans. Pro-Tito accounts tend to dismiss these contacts as no more than an attempt (successful) to arrange an exchange of prisoners: anti-Tito writers naturally consider them more sinister. German commanders on the spot seem to have been willing to let the Partisans get at the Četniks without interference, but Hitler was not prepared to have any dealings with pro-Communist guerrillas (he did not really approve of co-operation with Četniks either). The Russians also protested against contacts with the Germans, while the British, through their liaison officers with Mihailović, attempted to prevent Četnik co-operation with the Germans.

The Fourth Offensive in fact virtually destroyed the Četniks as a credible force outside Serbia, but it left the Partisans also, though temporarily, in a weak state, still seriously harrassed by pursuing forces and aircraft. At length they found a temporary resting place in east Bosnia.

One hopeful development was the growing contact with the British since Churchill had begun to take an interest in the Partisans; a liaison officer was parachuted in who was a personal friend of the British prime minister. This was Captain Deakin, who established a good rapport with Tito, helped perhaps by the fact that they were both wounded during the same attack not long after his arrival. A second British officer, Captain Bill Stuart, was killed on that occasion. Not the least of Tito's qualities as a leader of irregular forces was his luck. He had numerous narrow escapes but was never captured. The Germans offered a large reward for him, and so did the Italians (the Germans offered the same reward for Mihailović, but the Italians valued Tito at double Mihailović's price). Deakin was later superseded by a senior officer, Brigadier Fitzroy Maclean, another friend of Churchill and a Conservative Member of Parliament, and British supplies began to arrive in increasing quantities, though the Partisans felt there might have been more. Another encouraging sign was the Allied invasion of Sicily (leading to the fall of Mussolini), an occasion marked by Tito with a gift for the Allied liaison officers of a bottle of traditional plum brandy.

Things were looking up. The evident disintegration of the Italians and their Ustaše allies made it easier for the Partisans to reorganize and re-establish control in the west of the country. In September, Italy surrendered, and a race ensued for the arms of the Italian forces in Italy. The Germans gained the key Italian positions, but the Partisans managed to secure a good share of arms. Tito was very annoyed that he had not been advised in advance of the impending surrender, especially as he suspected that Mihailović had been tipped off by Colonel Bailey. This was not true, and the Četniks gained comparatively little from the Italian surrender. On the Dalmatian coast, Partisans and nationalists co-operated for a time, as they had in Slovenia, but the Germans soon regained control of that vital area.

Already, Allied propaganda was swinging around to Tito. In wartime propaganda there are only extreme shades of black and white: Mihailović had once been described as though he were some kind of Yugoslav St George and King Arthur rolled into one; now he was becoming a villain of darkest hue, while Tito was given a quick coat of angelic white and pushed on to the pedestal from which his rival had been removed. At the Teheran conference in November, the Big Three (Churchill, Roosevelt and Stalin) agreed to give all possible aid to Tito's Partisans. In December Mihailović failed signally to perform two specific acts of sabotage requested by General Sir Henry Maitland ('Jumbo') Wilson, commander-in-chief Middle East, and a few weeks later British liaison officers with the Četniks were withdrawn. The Americans kept in touch with Mihailović for a time, but their man was eventually taken out after the British had complained that his presence was making Tito cross.

As a sign of his strength, Tito felt able in November 1943 to set up a provisional government – a direct challenge to the royalist government in London – with Tito himself as president. It took a moderate stance: the question of the monarchy, for example, was to be left to a vote of the people after the war had ended. But there was little doubt which way the wind was blowing. Mihailović retaliated with his own constitutional congress in a village in west Serbia in January 1944, but it counted for little. In Serbia, many people had been angered by the Allies' rejection of Mihailović, but the Četnik leader had been ruined by the sectarianism which he had never managed to overcome and by his acceptance of the nominal leadership of collaborationists. Outside Serbia, or at least outside the Serb nation, he never commanded the support he needed if he were to lead a truly Yugoslav challenge to the Communists.

Although hard times still lay ahead, the Partisans were never threatened with extinction again after the Italian surrender. Allied assistance increased, and in January American and Russian missions arrived at Tito's headquarters. The leader of the Soviet mission was General Korneev, a fat and elderly person encased in heavily gilded dress uniform. His staff brought with them a large quantity of liquor, rumoured to be rather a weakness of the General's, and lost no time in complaining that the latrines were substandard. Soon afterwards, the Partisans sent their own mission to Moscow. It was led by Djilas, who gathered there the material for his well-known book, *Conversations with Stalin*. Warnings were uttered that neither Churchill nor Roosevelt were to be trusted; but, as Tito remarked on one occasion, it was the British rather than Russians that kept him supplied. Some 15,000 tons were dropped in the first six months of 1944 (up to June 1943 the total was $6\frac{1}{2}$ tons) as well as tanks and planes sent by sea, and over 10,000 wounded were evacuated by air to hospitals in Italy.

The improved position of the Partisans was reflected in a flood of new recruits, notably many Croats, giving what had originally (like the Četniks) been predominantly a Serbian organization a more Yugoslav aspect.

The Germans responded with a renewal of operations against the guerrillas designed to safeguard the areas in which they were chiefly interested–the district around Belgrade, the Morava valley and the Dalmatian coast. Most of the islands had fallen to the Partisans, and the Germans feared they might form a springboard for an Allied landing in the Balkans. In a short time the Germans regained control of most of the islands, but not the island of Vis, where Tito was shortly to make his headquarters.

What convinced Tito that the time had come, much as he disliked the idea, to set up a safe and permanent headquarters and to give up his peripatetic and hazardous existence with his troops was a narrow shave at his base in Drvar on 25 May. Drvar was a small industrial town in Bosnia, on a railway line, with mountains to the north and south, occupied by two or three divisions of Partisan troops. Tito's headquarters were in buildings erected inside a natural cavern on the hillside, virtually impregnable. These seemingly satisfactory arrangements probably led to a certain complacent relaxation of their guard by the Partisans, who were completely surprised by the dawn attack of 500 SS paratroopers, followed by more German troops in gliders. The town was captured after a fierce fight that lasted all day, and Tito escaped by the skin of his teeth through a hole in the floor of his headquarters and down a rope to the stream running below. With a very small party, which included the British and Soviet missions, he made off through the woods, temporarily out of contact with his forces and sometimes only a step ahead of the Germans. Urged to put himself out of danger by the Russians, he was evacuated by aircraft to Bari in Italy, which had become the base for Allied operations in the Balkans. There he had some discussion with British commanders and returned, on a British destroyer, to the island of Vis. After dinner in the destroyer's mess, this remarkable man entertained the company with a recitation, in very broken English, of 'The Owl and the Pussycat'.

Tito's position vis-à-vis the Western Allies was further strengthened by the approach of the Red Army during 1944. In London, meanwhile, pressure had been put on the Yugoslav government in exile to get rid of Mihailović and attempt to come to an amicable agreement with Tito. Churchill put some fairly heavy pressure on the young King, and a new government was formed headed by Ivan Šubašić, who had long been advocating an approach to Tito. Šubašić visited Tito on Vis and found him, though not unreasonable or intransigent, not very accommodating either.

Fighting between Četniks and Partisans increased as the latter attempted to regain some authority in Serbia. In spite of his rejection Mihailović, who never fully comprehended that the British and the Americans were really and truly allies of Stalin's Communist state, continued with care and devotion to rescue Allied (mostly American) airmen and return them to safety.

In September, a decisive month, Tito met Churchill at Caserta. Although they did not speak the same language – and in more than one sense – they nevertheless, and perhaps predictably, found in each other personal characteristics to which they responded warmly. But Tito annoyed the British leader soon afterwards by suddenly leaving Vis, 'levanting', as the testy Churchill put it, without a word, en route for Moscow. Meanwhile the Red Army entered Yugoslavia from Rumania and Bulgaria. As elsewhere, there was to begin with friendly co-operation between the front-line Soviet soldiers and the native irregulars, Mihailović's men, but this soon changed. The Četniks then were disarmed, and Titoist authorities set up in the liberated towns.

There had been many strange conflicts going on in the country since 1941, but nothing stranger than Serbia presented in the autumn of 1944. As Stevan K. Pavlowitch describes it, 'the Bulgarian army returned, to help liberate, under Soviet command, the territories which they had helped occupy, under German command, until just over a month before . . . for a short spell Soviet troops were co-operating with Mihailovićhist guerrillas against the Germans; Bulgarian troops co-operating with Titoist guerrillas against Mihailovićhists; Titoists fighting both Mihailovićhists and Germans'. (*Yugoslavia*, Benn, London 1971, page 165.) Mihailović was forced to withdraw to Bosnia but, after the liberation of Belgrade (20 October) the Red Army moved on into Hungary, and the Germans were able to retrench, checking the advancing Partisans on the Slavonian Plain west of Belgrade. Mihailović offered to place his men under Allied command, to fight anywhere against the Germans, but his offer was not accepted. There was some suggestion of the Četniks again joining the Germans to fight against the Partisans, but that plan also was rejected.

At a meeting in Moscow, Churchill, in the casual way of statesmen on the winning side in a war, had tossed across the table to Stalin a note suggesting that, as part of the arrangement of post-war Europe, Great

Power influence in Yugoslavia should be divided fifty-fifty, whatever precisely that implied. In line with this agreement (though naturally, when he heard about it, he resented it) Tito agreed to a provisional government to include non-Communists and a postwar constitutional referendum to decide other issues, such as the monarchy (Stalin advised Tito to have the King back, pointing out that he could always stick a knife in his back at some later date). Tito was making no great concessions, for it turned out that he was prime minister and minister of defence in the provisional government while the great majority of other ministries were held by Communists.

It was not until late March that the final withdrawal of the Germans from Yugoslavia got under way. Many people retreated with the Germans rather than fall into the hands of the Partisans, but Mihailović, preparing to begin the struggle again against a new opponent (if, indeed, Tito had not been his chief opponent all along), remained in Bosnia with rapidly dwindling support. The Partisans raced to occupy Trieste, which they hoped to include in the new Yugoslavia, and reached it a day or two ahead of New Zealand forces, breaking off their fight with the Germans (who were proving very reluctant to surrender to irregular forces) in order to go around them to reach Trieste first. After a few tense days, Tito was forced to withdraw, Stalin giving only half-hearted (fifty-fifty?) support to his claim that Trieste and Istria were rightfully part of Yugoslavia. The remaining German forces in Yugoslavia surrendered on 15 May, six days after the general surrender terms had been ratified in Berlin. The civil war continued a little longer but by the end of May Mihailović had only 2,000 men left, and they were soon rounded up. Subsequently, Mihailović was tried as a collaborationist, convicted and executed.

Above: Women sometimes fought alongside the Greek guerrillas; more often they played a supporting role to the various partisan groups.

Below: The Germans interrogating the mayor of a Cretan village; Crete was a centre of resistance work throughout its occupation.

Greece

In occupied Greece, as in Yugoslavia and Albania, militant resistance to the enemy was merely one aspect of what became an internecine struggle in which the main consideration was not getting the occupiers out but acquiring power when they left. The guerrillas in the mountains, whether they knew it or not (the majority at first did not), were engaged in a civil war; but, just as that was not realized by the villagers and shepherds who bore the brunt of the violence, it was of comparatively little interest, at least until fairly late, to the powers outside Greece, notably the British government, who attempted to direct and supply the guerrilla forces.

Without attempting to describe, even briefly, the tortured political history of Greece before the Second World War, it can be said that in the generation before 1940 there was a basic power struggle between monarchists and republicans, in which kings came and went (at one point a father succeeded his son on the throne) and parliamentary democracy failed lamentably to give the state anything like a decent government. Personal feuds and the economic slump of the early 1930s, which hit Greece particularly hard because its export trade was mainly in luxury items that had to be sold in order to pay for imported necessities, made Greece appear a rather miserable place to live in, although ten years later the early 1930s appeared a golden age by comparison with the current situation.

In 1935 an attempted coup by republican army officers provoked a conservative, royalist reaction, the return of King George II, and the appointment of General John Metaxas as minister of defence–leading to reforms that made the army vastly more efficient. In parliament, however, the political situation was the familiar one of stalemate–the bickering of special interests and the irreconcilability of political opponents again making firm government impossible. One disturbing factor was the influence of the Greek Communist party, known by the initials of its Greek name as the KKE (the proliferation of organizations identified by more or less enigmatic groups of letters, which was a notable by-product of the war, was especially rich in Greece). Although very small, the KKE was extremely well organized, and chance made it influential beyond its representation in parliament because potentially it controlled the balance of power. Against this background, rumours of an impending Communist-organized general strike provoked a coup in August 1936, the effect of which was to make General Metaxas dictator of Greece. Although he led a party that was even smaller than the KKE, Metaxas had come to power by the fortuitous death of the prime minister and his immediate deputy. He was able to persuade the king to sign the decree giving him absolute powers (a signature which perhaps, looking far ahead, also consigned the monarchy to extinction), and set about giving Greece what it certainly needed, strong government. Dictatorship in the 1930s, however, generally included some highly unpleasant aspects, such as persecution of the left, a powerful secret police, and a propagandistic youth movement. All these were characteristic of Metaxas's rule and although his regime was less brutal than that of Mussolini—and to compare him with Hitler would be absurd—he was not popular. It was perhaps the unpopularity of the Metaxas regime, rather than his highly effective improvement of the armed forces, that was uppermost in the mind of Mussolini when he ordered the invasion of Greece on 28 October 1940.

Although it was not preceded by a declaration of war, the Italian attack was not altogether unforeseen. The atmosphere had been strained since the Italian fleet had bombarded Corfu in 1923, an incident sorted out by the League of Nations, and in 1938 Mussolini's troops had made concrete the Italian control of Albania, which had been strongly under Italian influence since the Great War. This step towards a new 'Roman Empire' had made Metaxas redouble his efforts to make the Greek fighting forces ready for battle, and when the Italians seized on a minor border incident to make demands of the Greeks which included Italian occupation of some Greek territory, war became certain. Without waiting for Metaxas to reject his ultimatum, Mussolini ordered his troops into Greece. They received, however, a nasty shock.

To begin with, the Italians advanced, but rather more slowly than planned and against steadily stiffening Greek resistance. After a little more than two weeks, the advance petered out, and the Greeks began a counter-attack. One brave division managed to cross the Pindus Mountains and attack the Italians' undefended flank. Though much better equipped, the Italians lacked the fierce patriotic zeal of men defending their country against an aggressor, and they fell back rapidly. The Greeks chased them back to the border and advanced some 50 kilometers into Albania before a more or less stable front was formed which lasted throughout the winter—a cold one in which soldiers on both sides suffered from severe frostbite and food shortages. During that winter, Metaxas died in Athens.

Like the Finns against the Russians, the Greeks had performed far better than anyone could have anticipated, thanks largely to the mood of patriotic unity which made the imprisoned secretary of the KKE send instructions to party members to co-operate fully with the Metaxas government against the Fascists. In April 1941 the Germans, intent first on securing the whole Balkans area for their campaign in the east, and secondly on communications with the Afrika Korps, entered the fray. They swiftly rolled back the Greeks, as well as the recently arrived and meagre British forces, who evacuated the country after little more than a month, leaving much of their heavy equipment behind. Athens fell to the Germans before the end of the month. By the second week of June, following a daring airborne attack, the Germans were in possession of Crete. Having fled first to Crete, the king and remnants of the government removed to Cairo (George II subsequently spent most of the war in London, where he had the support of Churchill though not of all Churchill's colleagues and subordinates). A puppet government was set up by the Germans in Athens.

As in Yugoslavia, the Germans could not spare the troops to garrison the conquered country. Except for Crete and one or two other strategic areas, they quickly pulled out, leaving the country to their allies, the Bulgarians, who acquired some territory – permanently, they hoped – in Macedonia and Thrace, and the Italians. The fact that the Italians formed the major occupying force in the country undoubtedly contributed to the strength of resistance. The Greeks felt, with reason, that they had given the Italians a beating and that Mussolini's men would never have achieved their position as the rulers of Greece if it had not been for the German intervention. They were incensed at being subjected to a people whom they not only disliked but despised.

However, at first the new government seemed to the ordinary Greek (who, unlike the ordinary Athenian, is not entirely obsessed by political affairs) little different from the old. The Germans wanted no trouble in Greece and hoped for co-operation from the conquered inhabitants; both they and the Italians maintained a relatively 'low profile', and resistance was slow to materialize. The economic situation also militated against the immediate organization of resistance, for the agricultural disruptions caused by war greatly aggravated what was already fast becoming a chronic food shortage, and famine was widespread. Many people died, directly or indirectly, of starvation during the winter of 1941-42. The situation improved somewhat in 1942, partly as a result of Red Cross famine relief and partly through the economic stimulus of war, which created more work and higher wages until the paper money printed to pay the labour caused sharp inflation, leading to more hardship, in 1943-44.

Although not thickly forested, Greece's mountainous terrain makes it suitable for guerrilla warfare. The mountains, especially in the Pindus range, are rugged and remote; even in peacetime they sheltered bandits. Roads are scarce, and many villages can be reached only by mule or on foot: a full day's travelling by a guerrilla band averaged only about ten miles. Even a regime far more efficient and more popular than that supported by the Italians would have found it a hard task to keep a grip on the remoter areas of rural Greece. In the summer of 1942 there were many more or less unorganized guerrilla bands in action, some operating spasmodically, a few in permanent residence in the mountains. As in other countries, they included – besides patriots – criminals, adventurers, outlaws and others who for one reason or another had little choice except to join an outlaw band. Most of these guerrillas soon came under the control, real or nominal, of one or other of the two main partisan organizations, ELAS and EDES.

The initials ELAS stood for National Popular Liberation Army but had the advantage of sounding the same as the Greek name for Greece. ELAS was the military arm of the political organization EAM (National Liberation Front) and together they represented the extreme left of the resistance movement. The great majority of ordinary members of ELAS, as of similar popular movements in other countries, were not ruled by any particular political dogma but became members simply because ELAS was the dominant organization in their area, and a few of the leaders of the movement were not Communists. Although their Communist affiliations were played down and their propaganda emphasized patriotism rather than party, it was no secret that the dominant military personality in ELAS, Aris Veloukhiotis (real name, Klaras), was a Party member.

Aris, whose *nom de guerre* might be loosely translated 'the Mars from the Mountain' was a sinister figure of a type that is always likely to appear in times of war. His ability as a guerrilla leader is undoubted, though he spent much more of his time between 1942 and 1944 fighting fellow-Greeks rather than Germans or Italians, and many who met him paid tribute to occasional graciousness, while also remarking on the streak of savage cruelty in his character which made him employ pointless torture on his victims. He had been in prison under Metaxas but escaped during the German invasion in 1941 and the following year raised his first guerrilla band in the Pindus Mountains. Stocky, black-bearded, grim-faced except when alcohol made him amiable, and given to exotic black uniforms decorated with skull and crossbones, Aris was then in his early thirties.

General Napoleon Zervas, leader of the rival organization EDES, was some twenty years older, and a more attractive character. His courage, like that of Aris, was unquestioned, and his background was left-wing (though under pressure he was later to veer to the right.) A career soldier, he had been involved in republican politics in the 1920s, sometimes of an unethical kind, and had later been forced out of the army, whereupon he became involved in the Athens underworld. He had not fought in the campaign against the Italians, apparently because Metaxas had refused to allow him to serve in the army again, but after the German conquest he was associated with other republican officers in creating the underground political organization known as EDES (Greek National Republican League). In June 1942 he left Athens to take over command of the military wing of the movement in the mountains. Subsequently, Zervas's EDES guerrillas became virtually divorced from the parent organization, which 'remained little more than a cabal of ambitious politicians or would-be politicians in Athens' (William H. McNeill, *The Greek Dilemma*, London 1947).

EDES remained a much smaller organization than ELAS, never numbering more than 5,000 or 6,000 men while ELAS, by the end of 1943, could claim four times that number, and it was confined to the north-west, separated from the rest of the country by the Pindus range. It was thus difficult for Zervas to expand his forces, and ELAS eventually came to control virtually all partisan activity in the rest of the country.

In the early days, however, there were a number of smaller guerrilla groups in the field. EKKA (National and Social Liberation), led by Colonel Dimitri Psaros in the field, was politically a somewhat dilettantish centre-leftist group with intelligence contacts in Athens very useful to the British. As a military unit, it numbered only two or three hundred and was hemmed in by hostile ELAS forces which eventually forced its disband-ment, Colonel Psaros and his senior officers being killed – the sole fate, C. M. Woodhouse remarked, possible in the circumstances for 'the only guerrilla commander who was . . . an officer and a gentleman' (*Apple of Discord*, London 1948). Another prominent figure associated with EKKA was Euripides Bakirdjis, who went over to ELAS early in 1944 and later became president of the shadow government set up by EAM-ELAS.

Except for EKKA, none of the other minor guerrilla groups, mostly led by unemployed army officers, were acknowledged by or received aid from the British, and although several had some political significance their military units were all swallowed up by ELAS in 1943-44.

Almost from the beginning the British were in touch with the two main guerrilla groups, though they knew little about their aims, composition or method of operation, and were certainly not aware of the Communist influence in ELAS. In the summer of 1942 a small British group led by Brigadier Edmund ('Eddie') Myers with Colonel Christopher M. ('Monty') Woodhouse, who had already spent a year in occupied Crete, as his second-in-command were parachuted into Greece. Except for Woodhouse and a couple of radio operators, the group were intended to make contact with the guerrillas in order to carry out a specific sabotage operation, following which they were to be picked up from the coast by submarine.

As these things usually are, the whole operation was a skin-of-the-teeth affair. The first flight was aborted when the signal fires that the guerrillas were supposed to light could not be seen. Forty-eight hours later they were still not evident, but part of the team, in two of the three Liberators, dropped anyway (most of them had only a couple of days parachute training, hardly sufficient for dropping into alien, occupied, mountainous countryside by night with parachutes of a type they had not seen before). However, after some groping about, the whole team was reunited and soon made contact with both Zervas and Aris.

*Top left: Major George Agoros, a typical
EDES officer, with a civilian friend.*

*Top right: John Metaxas, pictured here
in 1936, greatly increased his prestige by
leading the opposition to the Italian
invasions.*

*Above: A group of women carrying
stores to a partisan hideout in NW
Greece.*

156

The central span of the Asopos Viaduct was blown up by a British team in June 1943, cutting the railway to Athens for four months.

The object of the exercise was to break the railway communications through Greece which were supplying Rommel in North Africa, thus aiding Montgomery's El Alamein offensive (as things turned out, the decisive battle was over before the railway line was cut). There were three railway viaducts which offered possibilities, but an inspection revealed that only one, the Gorgopotomos Bridge, offered a reasonable chance of success. That was accordingly the target selected.

Not the least significant aspect of the raid on the Gorgopotomos Bridge was that it was virtually the only occasion on which the forces of EDES and ELAS co-operated against the Axis. The political grip of the KKE had not yet tightened fully, and both Zervas and Aris were present, along with Myers. That raised certain difficulties about who was in command, which heightened tension, though without causing disaster. The viaduct was nearly 200 metres long, and it was necessary to send separate groups to attack the Italian guardposts at each end. Smaller parties were sent to cut the line a mile or two from the viaduct to prevent reinforcements arriving before the demolition was completed. The main demolition party, commanded by Colonel Tom Barnes, a New Zealander, was to act independently, placing 400 pounds of plastic explosives (brought from Cairo by the British parachutists) in the steel piers.

The attack was carried out successfully, though not without alarms and casualties. At one end of the viaduct the Italian defences proved to be better armed than expected, and it was necessary to throw in the meagre reserves at an early stage. Zervas, in the headquarters group, was concerned that ammunition would run out, and he was with difficulty persuaded not to give the signal for withdrawal before all the charges had been placed. Colonel Barnes's party, when they reached the piers of the bridge, found that they were not L-shaped in section, as had been believed, but U-shaped, which necessitated hurried reshaping of the plastic explosives before they could be placed in position. Nevertheless, they succeeded in planting their charges, lit the fuses, and sent two 20m spans of the bridge crashing to the valley below. Having had no sleep that night, the guerrillas withdrew through the fir forests, protected from pursuit by heavy snow. Myers's party then made their tortuous way to the coast, in weather now bitingly cold and wet, to the spot where they hoped to be picked up by submarine. But the submarine never appeared, and eventually a signal from Cairo reached them which requested that they remain in Greece to co-ordinate further guerrilla operations. They returned to Zervas, from whom they had so recently taken hearty leave, supposing that they would not see him again until the war ended. He greeted them with a touch of irony.

British liaison officers in Greece, though anxious only to co-ordinate resistance to the Axis, found themselves inevitably drawn into political conflict. It soon became apparent, to some of them at any rate, that EAM and ELAS were Communist-controlled and therefore not primarily concerned with action against the occupation, which was bound to be temporary, not particularly well-disposed to Britain, the arch-imperialist nation, and certainly suspicious of the British.

EAM-ELAS were becoming increasingly political or, rather, their leadership was; the ordinary people in rank and file were not, for the most part, politically orientated, and that is a fact which bears constant repetition. At every level of command, ELAS operated under a kind of triumvirate, consisting of the military commander, a political representative (commissar would not be quite the right word) and a *kapetianos*, a kind of moral leader who was also responsible for such matters as supplies. The military commander was, whenever possible, an experienced soldier. ELAS, far more than other organizations, was short of ex-army officers, largely because many army officers tended to be monarchists, or conservative republicans, and were therefore not trusted by EAM-ELAS. However, the actual power of the military commander was virtually non-existent, and it was therefore possible for ELAS to make use of officers who were not sympathetic to the political leadership. The military commander of ELAS was General Stephen Sarafis, who had a republican background admittedly, having been imprisoned under Metaxas. Originally, however, Sarafis had led his own independent group in the mountains, which had been soon encircled and overpowered by ELAS, until its commander was captured and, to the astonishment of observers such as the British liaison officers who were striving to prevent him being executed by his captors, emerged a few days later as ELAS military commander. It was assumed by the British that he was coerced, but in fact his conversion seems to have been voluntary.

Thus ELAS acquired a thoroughly 'respectable' military commander who never for a moment threatened the real control exercised by the other members of the triumvirate—the *kapetianos*, which was Aris, and the political leader in the field. Overall direction of EAM-ELAS came from the EAM central committee in Athens, then headed by George Siantos, who was acting general secretary of the KKE in the absence of Nikos Zachariadis, in a concentration camp in Germany.

The life of an ELAS guerrilla was usually a mixture of hardship and relative luxury; it was seldom as tough and unpleasant as the existence endured by—for example—many Russian partisans, and it was on the whole much easier than the existence of the ordinary peasant. Ammunition was usually in short supply, and so were clothes: when Brigadier Myers told Aris he was recommending him for a British decoration, Aris replied that he would rather have boots for his soldiers. Nevertheless, in the summer months at least, life could be rather pleasant. Lodgings were often requisitioned in the villages, and if it was necessary to sleep in the open that was not a serious hardship. In wet weather, ELAS men built shelters like wigwams from branches of fir trees. With bracken spread on the ground inside, they remained dry and comfortable. Food supplies were not always reliable, but food could be requisitioned (with payment sometimes, or promise of future payment). Hunger, even near-starvation, was experienced by Greek partisans, though for most of them it was by no means a novel experience. British liaison officers, perhaps benefitting from the strongly pro-British feeling evident in most Greek towns and villages (even, though more muted, after EAM became established), sometimes ate very well, perhaps not aware that they were receiving a special treat from hosts who were actually very short of food. In his book (*Greek Entanglement*, London 1955), Brigadier Myers pays handsome tribute to the constant courage and hospitality of the Greek people in the mountains and retails many a story of the generous treatment he and his comrades received: 'Some villagers brought us a marvellous meal. Denys [Hamson] ate five eggs without stopping ...' At Stromni, the villagers were especially kind, providing plenty of brown bread and potatoes, besides delicious apples, a speciality of the district. The occasional sheep could be purchased for gold, and a certain mountain herb provided an adequate substitute when the tea ran out.

Nor, for the ELAS guerrilla, was the danger of death or wounding very severe. A great deal of time could be spent lounging about adorned in cartridge belts looking and no doubt feeling like a tough guy, and there was just enough action–the occasional attack on a chrome mine or a railway line or a brush with an Italian column–to prevent the pose seeming false. Without detracting from the real hardship of living rough at high altitudes in wintertime, nor from the many acts of genuine bravery and self-sacrifice, it should be remembered that casualties from enemy action among Greek partisan forces were comparatively small: a larger number of Greeks died from enemy reprisals, famine and in civil war.

A significant part in the Greek resistance was played by the British liaison officers stationed with guerrilla forces. The British were interested only, or at least primarily, in winning the war against the Axis. Their policy in Greece was therefore to attempt to get the Greek guerrilla forces to unite in one body and to accept orders from Allied Middle Eastern Command. They failed in the former and had limited success in the latter. Probably nothing could have succeeded in uniting the opposing groups (except total support of ELAS against all others), though the British might have made a better attempt (Brigadier Myers, the senior British officer in Greece for about one year, had arrived having been told he was to lead a single commando raid before evacuation, and he was unable to speak Greek; in spite of his other excellent qualities, it cannot be said that he was well-prepared for the task he was unexpectedly given). The British wanted the Greeks to contribute to an overall strategic plan: they wanted them to lie low at one period, to blow up the Gorgopotamos Bridge at a certain time, to increase general sabotage activities at another time, and so on. In order to persuade the Greeks to fall in with these plans, which had nothing to do with the situation in Greece, the British relied on friendly persuasion—after all, they and the Greeks were on the same side—and the pressure they could exert by virtue of their position as arms suppliers to the guerrillas. ELAS was a good deal less dependent on British supplies than the British believed. It seems to have come into possession of the considerable quantities of Greek Army light weapons which were concealed at the time of the capitulation.

The British naturally found EDES a more sympathetic outfit. It was largely in answer to British requests that Zervas had taken to the mountains in the first place; he showed himself at all times willing to do what he was asked, even when contrary to his own interests, and he even went some way towards appeasing the British in his attitude to the Greek monarchy (favoured by Churchill), at the cost of appearing to compromise his own standing as a republican. Zervas, moreover, was a victorious commander in the Gorgopotamos operation, and he showed considerable tolerance in the face of aggressive acts by ELAS against his position in 1942-43. In spite of British efforts to create an agreement among all guerrilla groups, giving them their own areas in which other groups were not to poach, ELAS steadily absorbed or destroyed all rival groups, except EDES. But ELAS, unlike EDES so it appeared, was not content to fall in with Allied policy, preferring to fight the Axis in its own way and never losing sight of long-term objectives. EAM-ELAS leaders eventually signed a 'Military Agreement' which accepted the presence of British liaison officers but did not allow them to give orders, and which set up a Joint General Headquarters responsible to Middle East Command.

It was ELAS which, in spite of its leaders' complaints that Zervas was getting the lion's share, received the largest amount of British arms and supplies. The chief reason for this was the straightforward one that British policy, ostensibly though not always actually, was to supply any organization fighting the Axis, and since ELAS was the largest organization in Greece fighting the occupying forces it received the most supplies. In the summer of 1943, moreover, Middle East Command needed the extensive forces of ELAS in order to launch Operation Animals.

This curiously-named exercise was timed to precede the Allied invasion of Sicily. Its object was, by a sudden and sharp increase in sabotage, to convey the impression, probably shared by many Greek partisans, that the invasion was aimed not at Sicily but at Greece and the Balkans. To judge by German military documents, the operation was reasonably successful. One report, dated one week before the Sicily landings, regarded the sudden outbreak of sabotage as suggesting that 'a landing ... is imminent on the west coast of Greece'. During the summer the Germans greatly increased their strength in the Balkans generally, and the Greek guerrillas certainly played a part in thus stretching the enemy's forces thin.

The important railway line to Larissa was cut in several places by British teams supported by ELAS irregulars, and in spite of the apparent reluctance of ELAS headquarters, ELAS units carried out a number of

Opposite above: General Scobie (centre) at a meeting with Siantos (left) and Zervas on the disbanding of ELAS troops late in 1944.

Below: A money changer in Athens in 1944; there were at that time eight million million drachmas to the pound sterling.

Top: Mourners for the 23 members of EAM killed in a demonstration in December 1944 in Athens. The banner was written in the blood of the victims.

Above: Two former ELAS partisans lived as fugitives in Crete after being condemned in 1949 for their civil war activities, until they were pardoned in 1975.

useful operations on their own, such as an attack on a motorized column in a mountain pass which blocked the road so effectively that two German battalions were needed to flush the Greeks out and reopen the pass. The sabotage continued for a time after the Sicily landings, and the Germans could not be sure that a subsidiary landing in Greece was not on the cards. They continued to worry about this possibility until the autumn of 1944.

Instructions from Cairo after the invasion of Sicily were for sabotage in Greece to cease. Zervas obeyed orders as usual, and later took them perhaps a little too far by making an unofficial truce with the Germans. He was accused of treachery by EAM-ELAS, but they also had their contacts with the enemy at appropriate times. 'Collaborationists' is a term bandied about very freely in occupied countries, and the true extent of the collaboration, if any, is often almost impossible to judge. ELAS did not obey the order to cease all militant activity in July 1943, and continued to carry out what aggressive acts were judged desirable by its own leaders, with the result that the Germans mounted a number of anti-guerrilla 'sweeps' in northern Greece in which EDES as well as ELAS sometimes suffered.

Within the Communist leadership there were conflicting opinions on the desirability of co-operating with the British. The strongest argument in favour was the desire to establish ELAS as a force recognized by the Allied command, to counteract hostility from anti-Communist opinion in Athens and Greece generally, and allay the suspicion of army officers, whom ELAS needed to recruit. This desire prompted acceptance of the 'Military Agreement' and the setting up of joint headquarters.

The 'Military Agreement', and the successful Operation Animals which followed it, did not end the political difficulties in Greece. On the contrary, relations soon deteriorated. In August 1943 representatives of EAM-ELAS and other groups attended a meeting in Cairo (having been flown out of Greece in a Dakota) which ended in recrimination and resentment over the question of the constitution of the government-in-exile and the position of the king (both at that time in Cairo). The Greeks from the mountains were unanimous in demanding that King George II should not return to take up his crown unless a popular referendum had already confirmed the people's desire for a restoration of the monarchy. The King, backed by Churchill, resisted that undertaking. The guerrilla leaders returned disgruntled, and a few weeks later civil war broke out in Greece.

The collapse of Italy in September had brought ELAS a spectacular windfall in weapons. Some Italian units agreed to surrender to the Greek guerrillas provided they were allowed to keep their weapons and were treated as co-belligerents against the Germans. The Pinerolo Division in Thessaly surrendered under these terms, but a short time afterwards they were suddenly surrounded by ELAS units and forcibly disarmed. ELAS gained about 12,000 small arms as well as mortars, machine guns, and some pieces of mountain artillery. The Italians dragged out a miserable existence in the mountains as semi-prisoners.

Encouraged by the intransigence of the king, EAM-ELAS had already made the first moves towards setting up a provisional government. In the Pindus Mountains there was in effect an unofficial state by the summer of 1943, governed by the EAM Central Committee, with its own police force, a rudimentary taxation system, and a system of justice dispensed by 'People's Courts'. It was necessary to have a kind of passport in order to travel. Within this area the Athens government had no real power. It could not collect taxes, and its police ventured there only in large groups, even then not always with impunity. ELAS was not strong enough to keep out regular Italian or German troops, but when they approached, the guerrillas warned the villagers and both then melted away into the mountains, returning when the troops withdrew.

After the Italian surrender EAM-ELAS began to organize a regular provisional government, which eventually became known as PEEA (Political Committee for National Liberation). Its first president was Bakirdjis, though he was little more than a figurehead, the real power being held by Siantos, the minister for home affairs who was also the general secretary of the KKE. Although PEEA was not set up officially until March 1944, it existed in rudimentary form in the autumn of 1943.

At that time the EAM-ELAS leaders probably believed, in common with many others, that the liberation of Greece was imminent. The summer campaign of sabotage had fooled Greeks as well as Germans, and German troop movements in September, in fact caused by the need to plug the gap in Italy, seemed to indicate a German pull-out from Greece. This was one reason why EAM-ELAS were prepared to show their hand by attacking their rivals, an act which finalized the break with the British, perhaps inevitable after the failure of the Cairo meeting. Supplies to ELAS were cut off, and some British liaison officers found themselves virtual prisoners of the ELAS units to which they were attached (in other cases good relations were maintained at local level, always friendlier than at headquarters). One officer was subsequently killed by undisciplined ELAS personnel.

The civil war began in October with clashes between ELAS units on the one hand and nationalist guerrilla groups including EDES on the other. The fact that clashes occurred more or less simultaneously in all parts of the country is, as C. M. Woodhouse has pointed out (*The Struggle for Greece*, London 1976), in itself proof, if proof be needed, that ELAS was the aggressor; for no other organization had such wide coverage. The main conflict was of course between ELAS and EDES, in which the latter appeared very much the weaker. For although British supplies to Zervas had been increased, this did not compensate for the huge accession of arms to ELAS during the aftermath of the Italian surrender; Zervas had obtained only a few weapons at that time, and his forces were outnumbered by ELAS three to one.

Nevertheless, Zervas proved a tougher proposition than ELAS leaders expected. Moreover, it seems clear that EAM-ELAS leaders overestimated their own strength, perhaps misled by the grandiose labels of 'brigade', 'division', and so on which had been attached to comparatively humble ELAS units as part of the effort, probably tactically misguided, of turning ELAS into a regular national army rather than a guerrilla organization.

For all that, at one point Zervas seemed on the brink of extinction. When ELAS attacked, he was rapidly driven back towards the sea. He was desperately short of ammunition, and was soon penned into one narrow valley, with ELAS poised to wipe him out, and with virtually no means of resistance left. All depended on an arms drop from Cairo – but the weather was unfavourable. In the end, one aeroplane got through, and Zervas was saved. In fact, ELAS was soon faced with the same problem, being a long way from its bases, and was forced to retreat as Zervas launched a counter-attack. Across the Pindus Mountains – in the depth of winter – Zervas pursued ELAS, but once in the plains on the other side ELAS had better access to supplies and Zervas's momentum began to run out. By February, Zervas was confined again to possession of the same region as he had held before hostilities began. Meanwhile, both sides had suffered considerable casualties, in the case of ELAS between 500 (their figure) and 1,400 (the enemy's figure), to the Germans.

News of the civil war in Greece was swiftly known abroad, and world opinion was shocked by the conflict not only between two allies but between two resistance organizations in the same country. Much pressure was exerted to arrange a truce, and eventually an agreement was signed at the Plaka Bridge, with British and American representatives taking part. The agreement laid down the boundaries between ELAS and EDES zones and stated that both sides would henceforth direct their hostility only against the Germans. It was, however, only a truce, and in future Zervas stationed his strongest troops on the border of his zone ready to repel ELAS attacks.

More generally, the civil war had emphasized and increased political divisions within Greece. It turned Zervas himself, and many other moderate republicans, farther to the right. Some young anti-Communist army officers joined the German-sponsored Security Battalions or co-operated with the Germans in other ways, seeing the Communists as a greater menace than the Nazis now that the war seemed to have turned against Germany, and in any case disillusioned with the whole idea of resistance. (C. M. Woodhouse relates in a footnote to his book *The Struggle for Greece* how some friends in Greece in 1971 apologized to him for a comment in their local newspaper which described him as having been 'with the Resistance'.)

EAM-ELAS seemed to have lost nothing by the events of the civil war, or rather the 'first round' of the civil war as it turned out to be. Allied military thinking held that guerrilla operations in Greece were still necessary and desirable, and since ELAS was still the only organization able to conduct them on a nationwide scale, supplies were renewed. The idea was that, although a landing in Greece was now ruled out, the guerrillas could usefully harass the Germans as they withdrew in order to meet pressure elsewhere. But more than likely it was also felt that the Greek guerrillas had to be kept busy against the Germans or else they would once more start fighting among themselves. The resumption of Allied arms supplies and the establishment in March of the PEEA, which contained only a few card-carrying members of the Communist Party, helped to restore the credibility of EAM-ELAS as a patriotic organization.

In the spring of 1944, many Greeks, watching the might of Germany shrink visibly day by day, still hoped for and expected an Allied landing. But the landing never came, and as the Red Army marched into the Balkans it became obvious that the Germans would soon have to withdraw from Greece of their own accord or be cut off by the Russians. Rumours of the German withdrawal sprang up every day, and the slightest sign was interpreted as evidence that the order to pack up had been given. As in other occupied countries, the German regime had become nastier as time went on and it became apparent that the Germans were not going to conquer the world; there had been some fearful atrocities provoked, some said, especially in the Peloponnese where Aris had been active, by ELAS. The great majority of Greeks were therefore united in one thing—detestation of the Germans and delight that they were at last, at the end of August 1944, moving out. They were, however, united in little else.

EAM confidently expected to inherit power in Greece, and although members and sympathizers of EAM-ELAS numbered probably not more than 25 or 30 per cent of the population, there was certainly no organization that looked capable of offering a serious challenge. Nevertheless there were still places, not least in Athens itself, where it was still possible to speak a word against EAM without being arrested by them and charged with treachery. In the dying days of the occupation, it was difficult for those Greeks opposed to the aims of EAM to know what to do, and although there was still comparatively little open and direct collaboration, there was certainly a more tolerant, even commendatory attitude towards such organizations as the Security Battalions which offered some kind of counterweight to EAM-ELAS. Increasingly there was in Greece a gravitation towards extremes—the extreme left, represented by EAM-ELAS (controlled by the Communist Party) and the extreme right, represented symbolically by the king and including a vociferous and in the circumstances absurdly unrealistic imperialistic element calling for a 'Greater Greece'. The political centre hardly existed, though outside Greece it was represented by the new prime minister of the government in exile, George Papandreou, who presided over a conference in the Lebanon in May to set up a government of national unity, in which EAM participated. The EAM ministers in the new government did not in fact arrive in Cairo until September, and the PEEA was then dissolved.

By that time the liberation of Greece was under way. A token British force of 4,000 men under General Ronald Scobie was assigned to the task, which in fact amounted to nothing more than filling the vacuum left by the Germans and incidentally preventing ELAS from filling it. By the Caserta Agreement in September all Greek guerrilla forces acknowledged the Papandreou government, while the government put all Greek forces temporarily under Scobie's command. In fact both sides—EAM and the Communists, the conservatives and the British—were playing for time. EAM, though at first surprised by the relative weakness of the British force, believed that the future belonged to them.

The British forces could make no serious efforts to come to grips with the Germans. There were a few clashes with the German rearguard, and a brigade of paratroopers followed the enemy northward, snapping occasionally at their heels. Zervas harassed them somewhat in Epirus, and some ELAS units were also in action, though they seemed more interested in wiping out what remained of the Security Battalions (disowned by the Papandreou government) than in attacking the Germans.

British troops received a warm welcome in most parts, even in some places where EAM was dominant, but more so where they were seen as potential saviours of Greece from the Communists. By the end of October the liberation was complete and, on the whole, this tricky phase passed off smoothly. General Scobie had issued stern orders against mob justice, and though some collaborationists were murdered there were far fewer atrocities than might have been expected. Yet there was little cause for optimism. The economy, naturally, was in complete chaos, and explosive inflation had rendered the drachma totally worthless; commercial transactions were restricted to barter. But if the economic problems were staggering, the political outlook was even gloomier. After the initial euphoria, tension was soon rising fast, and the British paratroopers who had been due to return to the war in Italy were retained in Greece. EAM became restless when the leftward swing of the government which they had expected to occur once it was re-established in Athens failed to materialize. EAM retained control of much of the country, and staged provocative demonstrations in Athens, where the right was more evident.

The crucial question concerned disbandment of troops. Spokesmen on the right said that ELAS should be disbanded since the task which it had been created to perform—resistance to the Axis—had now been completed. EAM was not unnaturally reluctant to forfeit the control it had won over so much of Greece during the previous two and a half years, and said that it would only disband if the Third Brigade was disbanded also. (The Third, or 'Rimini' Brigade, was the loyalist remnant of the Greek Army in the Middle East, which had been purged following a leftist mutiny, with the result that it was solidly conservative and pro-monarchist). This the government–and the British, who were in fact calling most of Papandreou's shots–refused to contemplate (though some Communists maintain that Papandreou did make such a commitment but then failed to act on it).

What caused the final explosion is a matter of dispute. The ultimatum to ELAS to disband issued by General Scobie, and shortly followed by the resignation of all EAM ministers from the government, may have been the spark that lit the powder barrel, but probably civil war was unavoidable by the end of November. Whether it was actually planned by the Communists is less probable. Certainly, when violence began on 3 December, with an officially banned EAM demonstration getting out of control and several civilians being shot by the police (or, as Harold Macmillan and others suspected, by Communist *agents provocateurs* planted in the crowd), the rebels at first endeavoured to avoid clashes with the British. As late as 17 December Siantos allowed a British regiment to enter Athens unopposed, though by that time the British, under General John Hawkesworth, had become involved in the fighting.

ELAS never had much chance of defeating the British forces in Athens. In Epirus, however, they drove Zervas back to the sea and this time he could make no comeback: his men were evacuated by British ships. The appointment of the respected Archbishop of Athens as Regent, and the appearance of Churchill himself in Athens on Christmas Day led eventually to a peace conference and a truce. The 'second round', like the first, thus ended in defeat for EAM-ELAS, at least in Athens. The Communists retained enough power in the countryside to wage the 'third round' in 1946-49. Possibly the final round has not yet taken place.

*The city of Smolensk in flames in July
1941.*

Russia

In 1939 Hitler could not afford war with the West unless he felt secure in the east, and his remarkable diplomatic coup of August 1939–the non-aggression pact with the Soviet Union–gave him the security he needed. For some people the pact was a welcome resolution of complicated moral questions: 'everything had become clear. The enemy at last was plain in view, huge and hateful, all disguise cast off. It was the Modern Age in arms' (Evelyn Waugh, *Men at Arms*). In fact the pact was a temporary convenience, like the Munich agreement less than a year earlier, and both Hitler and Stalin originally viewed it as such. But there was another resemblance to Munich: Stalin, like Neville Chamberlain, wanted to avoid war so desperately that he convinced himself, against his own judgment, that he had genuinely bought not a temporary respite but a permanent peace. On the eve of the German attack on Russia, the Soviets were still conscientiously supplying Germany with vast quantities of materials about to be employed in fuelling the invasion.

Germany's rapid and extensive conquests which followed the non-aggression pact were not anticipated in Moscow, where they provoked considerable concern and apprehension. The Russians had made their own acquisitions in the wake of the pact, but the large buffer zone which they had created on their western frontiers could not be regarded as adequate against the sort of attack that the Germans had shown themselves capable of making in western Europe (and indeed proved entirely useless when the invasion was launched). Although it came as a surprise, there was plenty of advance warning of the German plan. Soviet intelligence had forecast it, and the British and Americans had advised Stalin of what was afoot in Berlin. German sources also were available to Stalin, and they at least could not be suspected of bluffing. Yet Moscow strove even harder to please the Germans.

The Soviet government did have good reasons for hoping, even against strong evidence, that war with Germany might be avoided. The Red Army was in no position to resist a determined enemy, as its poor performance against the Finns during the winter war of 1939-40 had demonstrated. Almost its entire command above the rank of brigadier, as well as a large number of more junior officers, had been annihilated in the purges occasioned by Stalin's paranoia. Most of its divisions were below strength and they were stationed in the newly acquired areas where defensive fortifications were incomplete or non-existent. Finally, considerable forces had to be maintained in the east, for fear of an assault by Japan.

Operation Barbarossa began on 22 June 1941 with three vast army groups attacking in the north, centre and south. Each of them broke through the Russian defences at several points within a matter of hours. The attack was even more successful than the Germans had anticipated, and it soon led to certain logistical problems. The Panzers so far out-raced the infantry, mopping up in their rear, that they were in danger of losing contact, and had to be supplied by air with the most ordinary supplies from bases over more than 300 km away. Behind the German front line were huge numbers, perhaps over 250,000, of Soviet troops, bewildered and even demoralized, but still armed and in some cases still in their units untouched by the advancing Germans. Although everything was in chaos, the Russians had not been definitively defeated. In Moscow, Stalin successfully asserted his authority as war leader (if it had ever been threatened), and on 3 July made a famous broadcast to the Soviet people, his first. In the course of a not particularly inspiring speech, he issued a call for guerrilla warfare against the invaders, demanding that the enemy be 'hounded at every step', and calling on the people to 'blow up roads and bridges, wreck telephone and telegraph lines, set fire to forest, stores, transport'.

Partisan warfare was less of a novelty in the Soviet Union than it was in many other countries. The civil wars following the revolution of 1917 had given many people experience of it, and there was something about guerrilla warfare that appealed particularly to Communist doctrine. In any case, there was a less clear distinction in the Soviet Union between regular and irregular forms of warfare, heightened by the fact that the Red Army was doing its fighting on its own territory, unlike Germans, British or Americans, and that as a result there was more interchange between partisans and military. Certainly Soviet authorities had, in the past, devoted more attention to the role of partisans in war than had most other national governments. Long ago – before the Nazis came to power in Germany – the Moscow government had commissioned plans for disrupting lines of communication, for forming small Communist Party groups around which guerrilla companies could gather and for establishing secret bases in the rear of an advancing enemy. Exercises for the training of partisans were planned at Kharkov in the Ukraine where the training included drill with foreign-made weapons, on the sensible grounds that partisans would have to depend on arms stolen or captured from the enemy. Aircraft and parachutes were also employed in this programme, and preparations were made for secret partisan bases along with the fortifications in frontier districts.

However, before the war began, partisan warfare had receded from the comparatively prominent position it held in Soviet defence thinking during the early 1930s, partly as a result of the disappearance of Y. K. Berzin, the military intelligence chief who had handled Communist espionage and sabotage in Spain before the Civil War and was executed during the purges in 1938. Of greater significance in making partisan war unfashionable were Stalin's pronouncements that Soviet frontiers were 'inviolable' and the Soviet state 'invincible', which discouraged plans for resistance to an invader–indeed, to give too much consideration to partisan warfare began to look rather like defeatism if not treachery. Moreover, Stalin was not unnaturally disinclined to promote the organization of local insurrection, which is what partisan action is, when it might be turned against his regime. So schemes for guerrrilla warefare were forgotten; supply dumps were stripped, and 'secret' bases abandoned.

When the invasion came, the old plans had to be hastily hunted out, dusted off and, if possible, put in operation. The first instructions for partisans, issued a week after the German invasion, were merely a straight reprint of instructions issued in 1919. As Kenneth Macksey has written, Stalin's broadcast calling for guerrilla activity was in a sense 'a cry of despair', an admission that the Red Army was incapable of holding the frontier against the Germans (*The Partisans of Europe*, London 1975). Nevertheless, his call had tremendous effects throughout Europe, greater (to begin with) in some other countries than in the Soviet Union itself. In the German-occupied countries the Communists who had, with some patriotic exceptions, been sitting uncomfortably on the fence since the German-Soviet Pact, began unreservedly the work of resistance. And they were often extremely good at it, being more experienced in the ways of propaganda and subversion than non-Communist resisters. A number had fought in the Spanish Civil War; many had training in paramilitary activities. Throughout Europe, the Communist Party became active in Soviet interests, and Soviet interests after Barbarossa included the support of all resistance movements, not merely Communist ones.

The Germans, as they advanced into Russia, were astonished by the general ease of their own advance but at the same time impressed by the valour–sometimes suicidal heroism–of many groups of Soviet troops. It was apparent that the Soviet Union was prepared to sacrifice far greater casualties in its defence than most other countries would have found acceptable. This was, or should have been, food for thought. The Soviet Union was astonishingly ill-supplied with practically every necessity for waging war bar one–manpower. The vastness of the country and its correspondingly large population were factors which in the end proved too much even for the brilliant *Blitzkrieg* tactics of the Germans.

In spite of the thousands of troops left milling around in the German rear as the Panzers raced onwards, there was very little partisan resistance at first. This was partly the inevitable result of a lack of planning and organization; but it is important to remember that the Germans, as they advanced into the Soviet Union, were not everywhere regarded as enemies. The Soviet Union is an association of many nations, some of which were (and no doubt are) both anti-Communist and anti-Russian. In the Ukraine there were many ready to welcome the Germans; to the Baltic countries which had but recently lost the independence they had enjoyed since 1919 or 1920, the Germans appeared as the means by which they might regain it. In these and other regions, there were many who were willing to assist the Germans actively by turning against the Soviets. It seems likely that in the initial phase at least, irregular warfare was a greater threat to the Russians than it was to the Germans.

Nothing better illustrates the essential stupidity of Nazi war leadership than the failure to capitalize on the chance to appear as liberators rather than oppressors in the Soviet Union. A great opportunity was pointlessly squandered, sacrificed on the ludicrous altar of Nazi racism. There can be little doubt of the widespread unpopularity of Stalin's regime, in Russia herself as well as non-Russian states of the Soviet Union, but the Germans failed to take all but the most limited advantage of it, until Himmler tried to do something about it towards the end of the war–far too late.

The Germans actually *created* anti-German resistance. Their attempts to provoke civil strife out of political, racial, economic or other differences were not unsuccessful, but often facilitated resistance and provoked hatred of themselves. Their brutal behaviour alienated thousands who might have been at least neutral, if not pro-German. The *Untermensch* view of the Russians was widespread and not confined to the SS. Ordinary Russian prisoners of war starved to death in droves; Keitel ordered 100 Communists killed for one German, while Himmler announced in a speech at Poznan that he would not care if 10,000 Russian women died digging an anti-tank ditch so long as the ditch was dug. Against such attitudes there was often nothing to do except resist. A Soviet officer grimly told Alexander Werth that, horrible though it was, the German treatment of Russian prisoners of war was actually an advantage to the Soviet Union, as it made Russian soldiers willing to fight to the death. There was occasionally available one other course of action–to join the Germans. Many Russians undoubtedly enlisted as *Osttruppen*, as the Germans called them, to avoid the horrors of German captivity.

As the German front advanced into the Soviet Union it became progressively longer, and the German troops were strung out ever more thinly. It was far from a single 'front' in fact, and could be penetrated in many places without great difficulty. At the same time, the area in the German rear grew larger and larger, and more and more difficult to control. Besides bands of leaderless men, the Germans had to leave much military equipment abandoned behind the lines. Operation Barbarossa was probably the largest single military operation in history, but the Germans' numbers, including their various allies such as Italians and

Hungarians, were not unlimited. Once partisan activity could be efficiently organized, it was clear from the start that the Germans would have a very hard task to suppress it.

On 18 July the Central Committee of the Party issued fairly detailed instructions for continuing the battle in the rear of the German advance. The main responsibility was put on local Party organizations, which were to prepare for resistance in areas likely to be overrun. Leaders were to be selected who were, by implication at least, good Party members; arms, supplies and cash were to be organized in advance and communications, by courier or radio, set up, although individual cells were to operate as far as possible in ignorance of others, with a single individual providing the link between one cell and the next.

Some Soviet partisan groups were not dissimilar in concept from the British Home Guard. They were often based on some local social institution, a village, a place of work, etc., and were up to 100 strong. The commander of one partisan company, quoted by John Erickson, relates how he was ordered by a local Party committee to form a company in the district covered by half a dozen villages at the end of June 1941. After a week spent in forming his company and providing some necessarily rudimentary training, the Red Army began to withdraw from the area, and he was able to gather arms from retreating units: 123 rifles and two light machine guns with ammunition. Three days later the area was evacuated, and his company went underground, taking shelter together with dispossessed civilians in the woods and becoming a recognized partisan detachment. During the six weeks following, the group carried out twenty-five 'diversions' in the enemy rear. They destroyed (according to their commander's report) more than twenty lorries and killed 'more than 120 Fascists', presumably alleged collaborationists as well as Germans, but at the end of that period they had only twelve men left.

Training centres for partisans were set up in August. They were staffed largely by NKVD (secret police) men, though the Red Army also provided instructors (in certain individuals the organizations overlapped). Instruction was given in explosives and demolition techniques and in parachuting. Candidates were carefully screened for political reliability by Beria's NKVD men, but the involvement of the NKVD, the Red Army and the Party in organizing partisans did not encourage a clear, central chain of command, and leadership at the top was often inadequate, a reflection of the chaos in the country at large. An underground leader in Minsk complained that he and others had been trying to set up a party group to carry on propaganda in the city, but found their work progressed only 'in bits and pieces [as] firm leadership is lacking'.

The main purpose of the partisans was to harass the Germans by means of sabotage, by (as one order put it) 'blowing up bridges and railway tracks, destroying enemy telephone and telegraph communications, blowing up enemy ammunition dumps'. Less was said about the assassinations,

*Industrial workers defending their
factory in Stalingrad.*

Above: The small single-engined planes used to supply partisans behind the German lines could easily be hidden in the woods.

Below: Soviet civilians were drafted for work on road-building by the Germans, under conditions that gave rise to much resentment.

carried out in great number, of collaborationists, alleged or real, including officials appointed by the Germans. Having to some extent covered the retreat of the Red Army from their district, the partisans went into hiding, and began their attacks on communications. They did not attack enemy troops, except very small isolated detachments. Within three months of the German invasion, the German command could no longer afford to dismiss the partisan threat as insignificant, although they inflicted no more than irritating pinpricks and certainly could not slow down the German advance. Moreover, in spite of the brutality of the SS on the one hand and the threat of retaliatory action by partisans on the other, in many places it would seem that the population at large was well disposed to the Germans.

Among the prerequisites of vigorous and sustained partisan activity are a sufficient supply of arms and ammunition and a fair degree of confidence that the struggle will not be in vain. Neither of these existed in the Soviet Union in 1941. Arms, and ammunition especially, were in very short supply, while the Germans appeared to be winning hands down. Railway lines cannot be blown up without explosive, and it must have been very difficult to raise enthusiasm for partisan activities while the Red Army was in full and calamitous retreat.

It is impossible to say how many partisans were actively engaged during the first six months of what in the Soviet Union is known as the Great Patriotic War. It is only clear that they were more active than the Germans asserted but less active than the Soviet authorities maintained. It is said that there were as many as 10,000 partisans engaged behind the German lines during the Battle of Moscow, but even if that figure is somewhere near the truth, it does not make plain how effective the partisan activity was. The Germans suffered considerable logistical problems, but it seems unlikely that the partisans made more than a small contribution to those problems. Stalin exaggerated when he spoke, in a bombastic speech commemorating the anniversary of the October Revolution, of German communications being 'constantly threatened' by partisans. More serious were the errors of the Germans themselves, their failure to allow for the effect on machinery and transport of extremely cold weather, or for the different gauge of Russian railway lines.

In December, however, when the German advance became at last bogged down while still a little way short of Moscow, the Russians managed to mount a counter-attack, and this first sign that the Germans were not to have everything their own way undoubtedly encouraged partisans, both actual and potential. The authors of Soviet propaganda found the partisans a rich source of morale-boosting material and there were many stories, embellished or not, of heroism and enterprise on the part of partisans during the Battle of Moscow. Zoya Kosmodemianskaya, an 18-year-old girl whose tortured and hanged body was found by a *Pravda* reporter in a village not far from Moscow in December 1941, became the famous heroine of national resistance.

Another advantage which, if not quite a prerequisite in partisan warfare is certainly highly desirable, is air support. There was virtually none in the Soviet Union until the end of 1941, when some supplies were dropped in Belorussia and other occupied parts. Having suffered terrific casualties to aircraft, with which they were originally quite well provided, the government could not afford to divert many to supplying partisans, but there was one particular aeroplane, a little two-seater trainer, as slow as a crow and with a range not much longer, which was quite suitable for making short hops behind the enemy lines and able to land on some very makeshift airstrips. These air supply trips were perhaps as important for their psychological effect as for the supplies they brought. They gave firm proof that the 'freedom fighters' behind the lines were not forgotten. Besides supplies, aeroplanes often brought in men–tough, loyal Communists who could be trusted with the difficult task of weaning the people from their acquiescence with German rule.

Without strong leadership, partisan bands easily disintegrated. They were more often than not hopelessly short of weapons and living in miserable conditions, perhaps with insufficient food, fuel or shelter, out of touch with superiors, and perhaps alien to the local population. In such circumstances, small groups tended to fade from the picture, but where organization was better and groups larger, they were in greater danger of being hunted down by the Germans. Even in areas where there was no collaboration with the Germans, there was often still greater dislike for Soviet partisans, whose behaviour could be as brutal as that of the SS. Vyacheslav A. Balakin, an 18-year-old partisan whose diary has been published in part, in the West (in *Soviet Partisans in World War II*, ed. John A. Armstrong, Wisconsin 1964), recorded his successful accomplishment of a mission to kill a woman who was the *wife* of a collaborationist, and betrayed no emotion except mild regret that three children were thereby orphaned. In Kharkov, the partisans polluted the water supply with the aim of causing an epidemic. In fact the plan failed, but if it had succeeded the local population would of course have suffered just as much as the Germans. In the Soviet Union as elsewhere, Communist partisans were much less inhibited by contemplation of the effects of their activities on the ordinary population. They were careful with their bullets, which were in short supply, but less concerned with human lives, which were not similarly scarce.

An incident reported by V. Glukhov in a book about Soviet partisans published in Moscow in 1960 is probably representative of many similar occurrences when partisans tangled with German troops. This particular clash took place in a village called Vesniny, where there was a sharp fight in which the Germans lost a number of men killed or wounded. However, they outnumbered the partisans and began to encircle the village, while the partisans were suffering that common plight of irregular forces, shortage of ammunition. They pulled out, leaving the village to the

Germans, who shot 200 people, mostly women and children, in revenge.

In his speech celebrating the twenty-fourth anniversary of the Revolution, mentioned above, Stalin made some remarks which, as Alexander Werth put it (*Russia at War*, London 1964), 'made perhaps a few Marxist-Leninist purists squirm on the quiet' when he spoke of the 'great Russian nation' and evoked heroic figures from the pre-Revolutionary past to inspire the present struggle. Stalin was always something of a nationalist at heart, and his speech was but one sign of a change of emphasis in propaganda and in war administration, in which patriotism became more important than Party, and ultimately the military gained an unaccustomed ascendancy over the political. (In 1942 the British were astonished to receive from Russia orders for a large quantity of gold braid. It seemed merely frivolous, but as a mark of the rising status of officers in the Red Army, it was more significant than the British realized.) An aspect of the growing prestige of the military commander was the apparent realization that the best guerrilla leaders tended to be army men rather than Party faithfuls. There were exceptions, of course, and it would be wrong to suppose that colonel and commissar were always deadly rivals; co-operation was common and many Party chiefs–for instance Khrushchev in the Ukraine–handled the army and the partisans with sympathy, appreciation and understanding.

The experience of other countries has not been that the best partisan commanders come from the professional military class. But in the Soviet Union, partisan warfare was different from what it was elsewhere. Partisan groups were more closely linked with the regular army and frequently operated in disciplined units. They often seem to have been absorbed into the Red Army without difficulty, though the individualism of partisans as a rule makes them less satisfactory as regular troops. Many Soviet partisan units really resembled commandos operating in the enemy rear rather than other resistance fighters in occupied Europe. Many partisan units of course *were* made up of regulars. One of the earliest effective units, formed near Kaluga in October 1941, consisted of the remains of an anti-paratroop battalion plus some escaped Russian prisoners of war. It gave valuable service during the Battle of Moscow but was wiped out after betrayal in January 1942.

During the fighting in Russia irregular forces were used by the Germans as well as the Soviet Union. In 1942 co-operation with the Germans was declining, though there were still many districts hopeful of German victory and, more significantly, there were various forces from within the Soviet Union fighting on the German side. Cossacks were used by the Germans as anti-partisan units. They were a savage lot, and were sometimes let loose by the Germans on a town they wished to terrorize (sometimes, apparently, in Red Army uniforms). Cossacks were not regarded, at least by the German army command, as *Untermenschen*, and since they were thought to have a tradition of hostility to Soviet

Communism, some more or less desultory effects were made to befriend them and to encourage them to enlist with the Germans. According to Alexander Dallin (*German Rule in Russia*, London 1957), over 20,000 Cossacks had joined the Germans by 1943. That is not, however, a particularly large number, especially as it includes those, possibly a large proportion, who claimed to be Cossacks in order to avoid German brutality. A far, far greater number fought in the Red Army (sometimes in cavalry units), and there were many Cossack partisan groups who took part in dangerous activities behind the German lines.

Also active against the partisans was the so-called Russian National Liberation Army, better known as the Kaminsky Brigade, and later an SS division. Kaminsky was a Russian of Polish descent, who had done some time in Siberia. Originally he was the leader of a band of perhaps 1,000 men in the forests east of the Pripet Marshes who were anti-Stalinist and, thanks to the Germans, better armed and disciplined than the average partisan unit. They wore a white arm band with the cross of St George and were at first used to protect German communications against sabotage. By the summer of 1942 their number had swelled to something approaching 10,000, and they proved very useful during the German offensive of that summer. They are perhaps best remembered for their savage activities when employed to assist in the suppression of the Warsaw Rising, when their behaviour was such that even the SS were shocked. General Guderian, the great Panzer leader known to his men as 'Fast Heinz', protested to Hitler about the behaviour of the Kaminsky Brigade, and Kaminsky himself was finally killed by the SS.

A much more impressive figure was General A. A. Vlasov, who appears something of a tragic hero (the resemblance to Coriolanus is marked). Of peasant origin, he was extremely tall, intelligent and charming. He had a distinguished military record and had been one of the heroes of the defence of Moscow. According to Khrushchev, Stalin considered appointing Vlasov to command at Stalingrad. But Vlasov suffered several disillusioning experiences in the field when, as he not unreasonably felt, he was let down by Moscow, and in the summer of 1942 he was taken prisoner by the Germans near Leningrad. Probably he deliberately allowed this to happen, though Captain Wilfried Strik-Strikfeldt in his memoir of the 'Russian Liberation Movement' (*Against Stalin and Hitler*, English translation London 1970) gives a different version. At any rate, so great was Vlasov's anti-Stalinism that it led him into the erroneous belief that nothing could be worse than the Soviet regime, and he offered assistance to the Germans as they prepared their drive into the Caucasus. He was appointed commander of the Russian Liberation Army (not to be confused with Kaminsky's similarly named organization), but in reality this was merely a grand name for not very much. Hitler was nervous of forming a substantial force solely of Russians, and the *Osttruppen* were not allowed to enlist with Vlasov. His army remained for two years more a piece of propaganda than

Above: Russian guerrillas rounded up by the Germans in July 1941.

Below: A group of Russian partisans learning to use gas masks.

Above and below: A traitor discovered and executed by Soviet partisans near Orlov, after they had successfully destroyed a German unit.

Above: Major-General Belov reviewing his troops behind the German lines in January 1942.

Below: A Cossack reconnaissance mission on the south Russian front in 1943.

a realistic fighting force, and it was not used in the front line. Yet in the opinion of some, Vlasov was an inspiring leader who might have worked wonders if he had been given his head. As things were, it was not until late in 1944, when the Germans were heading rapidly towards defeat, that Vlasov was put in command of all the Russian bits and pieces left on the German side and thus found himself with two divisions numbering altogether about 50,000 men. Some of them were then sent to fight on the eastern front where, perhaps by plan, they were badly mauled. Others, under Vlasov himself, went to Prague, where the war and, for a very large number, life itself came to an end.

From the end of 1941 onwards, the partisan problem for the Germans in Russia was an increasing one, and although it was not until 1943 that it became of real overall military significance, it was at times and in particular areas a considerable menace throughout 1942. East of Smolensk, in the area between Viazma and Yelnia, there was a particularly active force, said to number as many as 15,000, under the cavalry general Belov, another who had distinguished himself during the Battle of Moscow. A fair proportion of this force consisted of parachutists dropped behind the German lines to break up enemy communications, who were joined by local partisans.

In the summer of 1942 the Germans mounted an operation against Belov's forces under the command of von dem Bach-Zalewski, later commander in Warsaw. Some 40,000 German troops were involved, and the area to be cleared amounted to 10,000 square kilometers. Although the area was cleared all right, most of the Russians managed to slip out of the net before it closed. The Germans lost 2,000 casualties (though the partisans lost many more), and failed to capture General Belov, who was flown out in an aircraft sent for that purpose by Marshal Zhukov. For his men who returned with him after six months of almost constant action behind the enemy lines, Belov with difficulty secured just 72 hours leave; for the Germans were advancing again, though they were soon to receive a check at Stalingrad.

This was not the only anti-partisan operation of the Germans in the summer of 1942, preparing the way for their advance on Stalingrad and the Caucasus. In the forested area around Bryansk, good country for partisans, and in the country south of Lake Ilmen, the Germans conducted sweeps which, for a time, almost suppressed partisan activity. Hungarian and other non-German troops were used in these operations, but their success was only temporary. Because of the vastness of the country, the partisans were nearly always able to elude their pursuers. The Germans would sometimes enter an area which they knew to be the base for a large number of partisans only to find it apparently deserted. As they had, or so they thought, sealed it off, this was bewildering. And in fact the partisans often *were* there – hiding in small groups in the forest. When night fell, the Germans would be astonished to see flares popping up all around, signals to Soviet aircraft dropping supplies. The best that the Germans could do in the circumstances was to light flares themselves and thus obtain a share of the Soviet materials.

Besides that, they carried out frightful reprisals against the local population. It is said that when the partisans returned to a district in Belorussia from which they had been temporarily expelled by anti-partisan operations, they found that in their absence the Germans (or troops in German service) had virtually annihilated about 150 villages. Women, old men and children had been massacred, and the young men sent to labour camps. In the Soviet Union, horrors like those of Lidice and Oradour were a hundred times more frequent. A self-condemning document produced at the Nuremberg war trials, describing the results of an anti-partisan sweep in Belorussia in June 1943, listed 9,500 killed and 492 rifles captured. Allowing for the scarcity of weapons (less marked by this time however) and perhaps for the retrieval of some rifles by the comrades of the fallen, the vast discrepancy between human casualties and weapons suggested that the majority of those killed were not partisans. One particularly notorious brigade employed by the Germans against partisans in Russia and Poland consisted largely of violent criminals, including murderers. These men were let loose on helpless villages with the comfortable knowledge that whatever atrocities they committed, they would not be condemned or punished by their own superiors. 'The troops', went an order from Berlin issued in December 1942, 'have the right and duty to use any means, even against women and children, provided they are conducive to success ... No German participating in action against bandits [i.e. partisans] and their associates is to be held responsible for acts of violence either from a disciplinary or a judicial point of view'. (This order is quoted at greater length by Alexander Werth, *Russia at War*, page 724.)

The partisans lived – existed would sometimes have been a more appropriate word – under terrible difficulties. To avoid the Germans they often travelled distances which seem scarcely credible for men – and women – on foot, avoiding roads, and carrying loads of heavy equipment. They might be constantly on the move and, although they often took food from villagers without much compunction, they were sometimes near starving. There were few growing things that were not sampled – leaves, berries and bark. Hot meals were a luxury seldom experienced. How many partisans died from malnutrition and exposure it would be impossible even to guess, but there can be no doubt that it was a large number. There were few doctors available, no hospitals, indeed not the most basic first aid: the outlook for a wounded partisan was grim indeed (among partisans who eventually enlisted in the Red Army when 'overrun', one in five was unfit for military service). In some parts casualties from enemy action were high, but probably the largest single cause for declining numbers was desertion: it was a miserable, hard life, and the only compensations were companionship and sex–not sufficient motivation for many people. Hunger, wrote Basil Davidson, is 'a greater deterrent to resistance than all the measures of terror and arbitrary killing that were ever thought of' (*Partisan Picture*, London 1946).

Things were not always and everywhere so bad. In 1942, even while the Germans were advancing farther into the Soviet Union, there were considerable areas which were entirely free of Germans and ruled by the partisans. Indeed, the political role of the partisans was arguably no less important than their strategic role: they reintroduced Soviet rule, or kept its name alive, in areas where otherwise the effect of the German conquest might have made people much less inclined to return amenably to the Soviet fold. In the words of a Soviet history (*The Great Patriotic War of the Soviet Union*, Moscow 1974), 'Soviet people regarded the partisans both as a military and political force ... [they] embodied Soviet power in opposition to the cruelty and vandalism of the enemy'. In most occupied countries where there was guerrilla warfare against the Germans there were conservative elements among the resistance seeking to restore the status quo and there were also Marxist groups seeking revolution. In the Soviet Union, both functions were combined in the same partisan movement. As John A. Armstrong puts it, superficially 'the Soviet partisan movement appears to resemble that of a guerrilla force seeking to restore the authority of an invaded state [but] in many respects it was really closer to the guerrilla movements in countries where Communists are trying to build a new system on the wreckage of the traditional administrative and social structure.'

The 'partisan regions' (*partizanskie kraya*) existed in parts of the northern Ukraine which were forested, in Belorussia and around Bryansk. In Orel province there were said to be 54 partisan detachments with a total of 18,000 personnel, which controlled an area containing nearly 500 villages. According to Soviet sources, over half of the total area of Belorussia was in partisan control during the winter of 1942-43.

In 1943 the partisan war became a mass effort. As long as the Germans were evidently on top, the partisans were comparatively quiet, unable or unwilling to adopt too high a profile, but when the German advance came to a stop, partisan activity at once increased. The German defeat at Stalingrad had a profound effect on all Hitler's opponents, and the delay of the German spring offensive gave the partisans a better chance to become organized. If the Germans had any doubt about the expansion of irregular and behind-the-lines units they had only to listen to the air waves, for the partisans were now well provided with radios, and different units were becoming linked in an efficient network. From the spring of 1943 many, perhaps most, partisan operations were co-ordinated with those organized by the Red Army.

According to figures given by the Soviet historian B. S. Telpukhovsky (and quoted by Alexander Werth), the number of partisans in Belorussia during the eleven months after the momentous German defeat at Stalingrad were as follows:

February	65,000
June	100,000
October	245,000
December	360,000

(These figures probably include some refugees from the Germans who should not be counted as effective fighters; nevertheless, the numbers almost justify the use of terms like 'battalion' and 'brigade' often adopted by partisan units of more than a dozen or so.) The number of partisans in the Baltic states is said to have roughly quadrupled during the first quarter of 1943, and in the Ukraine to have increased two and a half times. Sabotage figures in Belorussia between August and November are given as: destruction of railway lines, 200,000; trains wrecked or derailed, 1,014; railway locomotives destroyed or damaged, 814; bridges destroyed or damaged, 72. This followed a call from Stalin for a special effort against communications which was known as Operation Concert (September 1943) and extended to regions where partisan activity had hitherto been slight. Total destruction during 1943 is given in another Soviet source as 11,000 trains derailed, 6,000 locomotives damaged, 22,000 lorries destroyed, 900 railway bridges and 5,500 road bridges rendered impassable, temporarily at least; the Germans were usually able to make good all but the most comprehensive destruction in a remarkably short time.

But the partisans were also active in actual fighting. One of the best examples of partisans acting in co-operation with regular troops occurred during the important battle of Kursk in 1943, which led to the reconquest of the Ukraine. Not only did the partisans play havoc with German communications, as the figures quoted above suggest, but they built bridges and cleared paths, which often required some fierce fighting, to give the advancing Red Army a firm foothold. During the Soviet offensive, partisans secured and held a number of vital crossings on the Desna, Pripyat and other rivers, as well as important railway junctions, giving valuable assistance to the vanguard of the Red Army. They also managed to occupy certain towns a day or more in advance of the army's arrival.

By this time the partisans were, of course, far better supplied with weapons and supplies than they had been two years earlier. Besides small arms and mortars, they had field artillery, anti-tank guns (with which they knocked many a locomotive off the rails), as well as explosives. They had developed some sophisticated methods of destruction themselves, including a demolition charge in chain form which cut a railway line in 500 places simultaneously. They also had better liaison, trained officers in command, sufficient food and medical supplies, and more doctors.

It is difficult to assess exactly how valuable the partisans were in the defeat of Germany by the Russians. There were special factors in the Soviet Union such as the more military character of many partisan activities, making it difficult to say whether a particular operation was 'military' or 'partisan', which made the situation more complicated. The partisans were never able by themselves to enforce a definite change of plan by the Germans, but they were sufficiently powerful to constitute a threat which the German planners always had to take into account.

Before the last German offensive, another attempt was made to sweep up the partisans in the region of Bryansk. The task was tougher than a year earlier, but the partisans still avoided being drawn into a direct confrontation. The Germans claimed to have inflicted extremely serious casualties on the partisans, though their figures seem decidedly optimistic; as before, the bulk of the Soviet irregular forces managed to slip through the net. When the German offensive did start, after considerable delay, it did so to the rowdy and nerve-racking accompaniment of bridges blowing and railway lines buckling, and small parties of Germans were frequently ambushed. The German operation soon had to be called off, and although by this time the whole strategic position had turned against the Germans, with the Red Army launching an irresistible counter-offensive in the Orel sector, the activities of the partisans in the German rear certainly played an important part in aborting what was virtually the last German offensive in Russia. One German general wrote that 'partisans are doing more damage to the *Wehrmacht* than anything else', but his statement should probably be taken more as an indication of the psychological effect of the partisans than of their true military significance.

Soviet sources imply that all partisan activity was more or less directly organized by the Communist Party: 'Millions of Soviet citizens responded zealously to the Party Central Committee's call for vigorous resistance behind the enemy lines [in 1941] . . .' Partisan groups are called 'Party organizations' in Soviet histories as if the terms were synonymous: Alexander Fadeyev was reprimanded for not showing that all resistance was directed by the Party in his novel *The Young Guard*. After the formation of a central partisan command in the summer of 1942, it was certainly true that a great deal of the organization was done by the Party, but the official Soviet view (which of course scarcely mentions the fact that a good many million Soviet citizens were better disposed towards the Germans than the Bolsheviks) disregards much spontaneous resistance. In the same way, Soviet sources tend to speak of the partisans as if they were equivalent to the regular army. This accords with Communist ideas of 'people's' armies, and it is true that the Soviet partisans were more closely associated with the regular troops than is usually the case and that, in 1943-44 at least, they were organized on military lines; but earlier in the war they were often out of touch with the Red Army, the nearest detachments of which might be several hundred miles away. Moreover, they had little of the equipment – or the weapons – of regular troops. It was not until 1943 that partisan activities came to be co-ordinated with the movements of the Red Army. Having prepared the way for the Red Army's advance by sabotage and other methods, the partisans were then overrun by the advancing troops and were themselves absorbed into the ranks of the army.

Besides the paramilitary operations of large partisan bands operating in traditional partisan style in the countryside, there was also, of course, urban resistance to German occupation in the Soviet Union, including all the activities common to resistance movements elsewhere, such as espionage, propaganda, sabotage. Among notable individual feats (there are numerous exciting, if often clearly over-romanticized, stories of Soviet partisans, as many as there are Western stories of wartime escapers) was the assassination of the governor of Belorussia, Wilhelm Kube, by a Belorussian girl, Y. G. Mazanik, who placed a time bomb under his bed. Western writers describe the girl as Kube's mistress, though Soviet sources speak of a partisan raid on the governor's residence. Another remarkable individual was N. I. Kuznetsov, a leader of the Ukrainian resistance, whose exploits included the assassination of an important German official by shooting, the killing of two other officials in another incident, and the kidnapping of a German general. Equally famous was the resistance group known as the 'Young Guards' in the town of Krasnodon, the subject of the novel by Fadeyev.

The partisans occasionally provided useful military information, but they were for the most part kept strictly separate from intelligence, chiefly because, in the days of German ascendancy in particular, the partisans were riddled with informers and traitors, or at least believed themselves to be. Partisan units were nevertheless used at times in a reconnaissance role. They were able, for example, to pinpoint the location of German headquarters or fuel and supply bases. This often continued when they were enrolled in the Red Army in 1943–44.

As the tide turned against the Germans, the numbers of partisans shot up and new recruits appeared daily; former supporters of the Germans hastily changed sides, encouraged by partisan leaflets which promised them one last chance to do so before they were exterminated (though a number of renegades retreated along with the Germans, including Vlasov's army). As they advanced, the Russians brought along more or less 'secret' armies to take over in the countries being liberated from German rule, like the Polish People's Army which the Soviet Union sponsored against the London-backed Home Army commanded by General Bor-Komorowski. In 1941 it had looked as though even some countries which had always been part of the Soviet Union might break away from Moscow's control. By the end of 1943 that no longer seemed possible, and it was beginning to look as though Soviet Communism would acquire a very much larger power base at the end of the war than it had enjoyed before the German attack of June 1941. This great reversal of fortunes might have been impossible without the partisans.

Index

Aarhus raid, 69
Abwehr (German military intelligence), 102
Albania, 13–24
Albert, King of Belgium, 93, 94
Alexander, King of Yugoslavia, 129
Algiers, 113, 115, 118, 120, 125
Alta airport, Norway, 81
Altmark, 71
Amery, Julian, 20, 23
Anders, General, 42
Animals, Operation, 161, 164
Antwerp, 99
Ardennes, 98, 99
Armée Secrète, Belgium, 98
Arnhem, 91
Astrid, Queen of Belgium, 93
Auschwitz concentration camp, 38

Bach-Zelewski, von dem, 56, 185
Bailey, Colonel S. W., 143
Balli Kombëtar, 17, *19*, 20, 21, 22
Bakirdjis, Euripides, 155
Banská Bystrica, Slovakia, 33, 34
Barbarossa, Operation, 17, 28, 133, 172, 173, 174
Barnes, Colonel Tom, 158
Bastia, Corsica, 113
BCRA, France, 104, 108
Belgium, 93–99
Belov, General, *184*, 185
Beneš, Edvard, 25, 26, 27, 28, 34, 35
Bergen, 72
Bernhard, Prince of the Netherlands, 85, 91
Berzin, Y. K., 173
Best, Captain Payne, 83, 89
Best, Werner, 63, 68
Blizna, Poland, 38
BOPA, Denmark, 63, 68
Bor-Komorowski, General, 46, 48, 49, 50, 51, 55, 57–59, 190
Bormann, Martin, 28
Bornholm Island, 69
Bosnia-Hercegovina, 136, 140, 141, 143, 147, 149
Bradina, Yugoslavia, 141
Bradley, General Omar, 125, 127
Brindisi, 23, 39, 40, 41
British Expeditionary Force, 101
Brossolette, Pierre, 103, 106
Brož, Josip, see under Tito
Bruijne, Colonel de, 89
Budapest, 34
Bug River, Poland, 39
Burza, Operation, 49

Caserta, *138*, 148
Čelje massacre, Slovenia, *128*
Četniks, Yugoslavia, *128*, 131, 132, 134, 135
Chamberlain, Neville, 13, 25, 84, 129
Chartres, 105
Christian, King of Denmark, 61, 62, 63, *64*
Chmielewski, Jerzy, 39
Choltitz, Dietrich von, 125, 127

Chrusciel, Colonel, 51
Churchill, Winston, 8, 21, 50, 101, 102, 103, 107, 130, *138*, 145, 146, 148, 153, 164, 169
CLNF, France, 104
CNR, France, 106–108
Combat, France, 105–106
Communist Party, Albania, 16, 17, 21–23; Belgium, 98; Czechoslovakia, 28, 29, 33, 35; Denmark, 62, 63; France, 101–107, 112, 120, 126; Greece, 151, 158, 159, 167–169; Norway, 80–81; Russia, 172–175, 179, 180, 189–192; Yugoslavia, 131, 133–136, 142, 146, 148, 149
Concert, Operation, 188
Copenhagen, 61, 62, *66*
Corsica, 113
Cracow, 38, 40
Crete, *150*, *163*
Croatia, 129–131, 135–136, 140–141
Czechoslovakia, 25–35, 129

Dakar, 103, 104
Dalloz, Pierre, 115
Danzig, Poland, 37
Darlan, Admiral, 113
Darnand, Joseph, 102
Davidson, Basil, 140, 187
Deakin, F. W. D., 140, 145
Dedijer, Vladimir, 136, 140, 141
Delestraint, General Charles, 106, 115
Denmark, 61–69, 71
Dewe, Walthère, 95
Drobnik, Colonel M., 49
Ducla, Slovakia, 33
Durazzo, Albania, 13, 16

EAM, Greece, 154, 159, 160, 161, *163*, 164, 165, 166, 167, 168
EDES, Greece, 154, 155, 158, 161, 166
Eisenhower, General, 35, 62, 99, 125
EKKA, Greece, 155
ELAS, Greece, *150*, 154, 155, 158, 159, 160, 161, *163*, 164–169
Englandspiel, 89, 90
Enigma cipher machine, 38

Fadeyev, Alexander, 189
FFI, France, 120, 126
Flanders, Council of, 99
FNC, see under LNC
Foča, Yugoslavia, 136
Forces of the Interior, Netherlands, 91
France, 101–27
Frank, Anne, *86*, 89
Frank, Karl Harmann, 27, 32
Freedom Council, 63, 69
Front de l'Indépendance, Belgium, 98, 99
Front National, France, 105, 106, 113, 125

FTP, France, 106, 113

Gabčík, Jozef, 29, *31*, 32
Garonne, 124
Gaulle, General Charles de, 102, 103, 105, 106, 107, *108*, 113, 125, 127
George II, King of Greece, 151, 153, 164, 165
Gestapo, 28, 29, 47, 49, 69, 73, 90, 102, 105
Ghegs, 14, 17, 23
Giraud, General Henri, 107
Giskes, H. J., 89, 90
Gleiwitz, Germany, 37, 84
Glières, France, 120
Golian, General Jan, 33, 34
Gorgopotamos Bridge, 158, 160
Greece, 151–169
Grenier, Fernand, 103
Grenoble, 114, 115
Grot-Rowecki, General, 48
Guderian, General, 181

Haakon, King of Norway, 72, 81
Hague, The, 83, 84
Haukelid, Knut, 75, 80
Hawkesworth, General John, 169
Heydrich, Reinhard, 28, 29, *30*, 32
Hitler, Adolf, 25, 28, 32, 33, 35, 37, 63, 71, 130, 165, 171, 181
Hoen, Pieter 't, *87*, 88
Holger Danske, 63, 67
Home Army, Polish, 41–49, 54, 58
Hoxha, Enver, 17, 22, 23
Hudson, Captain 'Bill', 142
Huet, Colonel, 119

Jongh, de, family, 95
Juliana, Crown Princess of the Netherlands, 85
Jutland, 68, 69

Kaminsky Brigade, 181
Katyn Forest massacre, 48
Khrushchev, Nikita, 180, 181
KKE, Greece, 151, 152, 153, 158
Korneev, General, 147
Kosmodemianskaya, Zoya, 178
Kossovo, Albania, 16, 17
Kragujevac, Yugoslavia, 134
Kruya, Albania, 16, 20
Kibe, Wilhelm, 190
Kubiš, Jan, 29, *31*, 32
Kuipers-Rietberg, Mrs, *86*, 89
Kupi, Abbas, 8, 16, 17, *18*, 20–23
Kuznetsov, N. I., 190

Lauwers, 89, 90
Leclerc, General, 127
Légion Belge, 98
Leopold III, King of Belgium, 93, 94, *96*, 98
Ležáky massacre, 32
Lidice massacre, *31*, 32
Linge, Martin, 74
LNC, Albania, 17, 20, 21, 22, 23

191

Lofotens raids, 74
Lublin, 40

Maclean, Brigadier Fitzroy, 9, 145
Macmillan, Harold, 169
Maquis, *100*, 107–108, *110*, *111*,
112–120
Masaryk, Jan, 28
Masaryk, Thomas, 25, 34
Mati Valley, Albania, 13
May, Ernst, 89
Mazanik, Y. G., 190
Mers-el-Kebir, North Africa, 103
Metaxas, General John, 151, 152,
154, *156*
Mihailović, Colonel Draza, 131,
132–136, *137*, 142, 145–149
Mikolajczyk, President, 48, 50, 51
Milice Française, 102, 120, 125
Milorg, Norway, 73, 74, *77*, 80, 81
Montagnards, Operation, 115
Montbéliard, France, 121
Montenegro, 130, 135, 136, 143
'Monter', 51, 54
Montgomery, General, 125, 158
'Motor', 47
Moulin, Jean, 105, 107, *108*
Munck, Ebbe, 62
MUR, France, 105, 114
Musée de l'Homme resistance
group, 104
Mussolini, 15, 16, 22, 146, 152
Muus, Flemming, 63
Myers, Brigadier E. W. C., 155,
158, 159, 160

Narvik, Norway, 71, 72
Naujocks, 38
Nedić, General Milan, 130
Nerevda River, 144
Netherlands, 83–91
Neurath, Konstantin von, 27, 28
NKVD (Russia), 50, 175
Noli, Fan, 14, 16
Nordling, Raoul, 126
Normandy invasion, 68, 81, 120,
124, 125
Norsk Hydro heavy water raid,
75–78, 98
North Pole, Operation, 89–91
Norway, 71–81

Okulicki, General, 49, 59
Oorschot, General van, 83
Oradour, France, *116*, 124
Orde Dienst, Holland, 88, 98
Oslo, 72, 80
Oslo Gang, 81
OSS, 7
Osttruppen, 174, 181
Overlord, Operation, 124

Palisad, Yugoslavia, 135
Papandreou, George, 167–169
Paris Uprising, 125–127
Parool, Het, 88
Partisans, 7–11
Partisans, Yugoslavia, 23,
134–146, *139*
Paul, Regent of Yugoslavia, 129,
139

Pavelić, Ante, 130
PEEA, Greece, 165, 167
Peenemunde raid, 38
People's Party, Slovakia, 32
Pétain, Marshal Philippe, 101,
102, 104
Peter, King of Yugoslavia, 130,
148
Pilsen, Czechoslovakia, 35
Pindus Mountains, Greece, 153,
154
Pinsk, 46, 47
Piwnik, Lieutenant Jan 'Ponury',
46–48
Poland, 37–59
'Ponury', 46–48
Praga, 51, 54
Prague, *24*, 27, 32, 34
Přikryl, Colonel Vladimir, 33
Psaros, Colonel Dimitri, 155

Quisling, Vidkun, 72, 73, *77*

Randwijk, H. M. van, 85
'Raphael', 39–41
Ravensbruck concentration camp,
32
Red Army, 171–172, 180–190
Red Orchestra, 95
Rée, Harry, 120, 121
Rexists, 93, 99
Rokossovsky, Marshal, 58, 59
Ronneberg, Lieutenant Joachim,
78, 79
Roosevelt, Theodore, 107, 146
Rundstedt, von, 81
Russia, 171–190
Russia at War, 180, 186, 187
RVV (Raad van Verzet), 91

St Nizier, France, 118
Sarafis, General Stephen, 159
Sava Valley, Yugoslavia, 140
Scamaroni, Captain Fred, 113
Scanderbeg, 13
Scavenius, Erik, 62, 63
Schalburg Corps, 68
Schreiber, Josef, 89
Schweik, the Good Soldier, 26
Scobie, General Ronald, *162*, 168,
169
Seraphis, General Stephen, 159
Serbia, 129–136, 140, 145–146,
148
SHAEF, 91
Shellhus raid, 69
'Shetland Bus', 74, *77*
Siantos, George, 159, *162*, 165,
169
Sicily, 161, 164
Sikorski, General, 41, 48
Simović, General Dušan, 130
Skinnarland, Einar, 78, 80
Slessor, Air Marshal, 54
Slovenia, 129, 130, 146
Smolensk, *170*
SOE, 7, 9, 29, 32, 62, 63, 68, 74,
78, 89, 91, 104, 120, 124
Sosnkowski, General, 48, 50
Spaak, Paul-Henri, 93, 94
Stalin, Joseph, 8, 21, 146, 148,

Stalin (contd.)
149, 171, 172, 173, 179, 180,
181, 188
Stalingrad, *176*
Strik-Štrikfeldt, Captain 181
Stuart, Captain Bill, 145
Subašić, Ivan, 148
Sudetenland, 25, 129
Sweden, 67, 68, 73

Teachers' Organization, Norway,
73
Tinnsjö, Lake, Norway, 80
Tirana, Albania, 13, 16, *18*, 20, 22
Tiso, Mgr Jozef, *30*, 33
Tito (Josip Brož), 7, 9, 23,
133–149, *137*, *138*
Tosks, 14, 17
Treblinka, 46
Trepper, Leonid, 95
Trondheim, Norway, 71, 72

Ukraine, 172, 188
Ustaše, Yugoslavia, 129–131,
140, 146
UVOD, Czechoslovakia, 28
Užice, Yugoslavia, 134

Valona, Albania, 14
Veloukhiotis, Aris, 154–159, 167
Vemork, Norsk Hydro raid, 75–78,
98
Venlo, Netherlands, 83, 84, 89
Vercours, France, 114–119
Vichy regime, 102–104
Viest, General Rudolf, 33, 34
Vis Island, Yugoslavia, 147, 148
Vlasov, General A. A., 35, 181,
185, 190
Vrij Nederland, 85, 88

Waffen-SS, 38, 46, 124, 181
Warsaw, 38–49
Warsaw Ghetto Rising, 43, 46, 55,
56
Warsaw Rising, *45*, 50, 51, *52*, *53*,
54–56, 59, 181
Werth, Alexander, 180, 186, 187
'White Rabbit', 106, *108*
Wilson, General Sir Henry
Maitland ('Jumbo'), 146
Winkelman, General, 85
Woodhouse, Christopher M., 155,
165, 166
'Woodpecker', 59

Yeo-Thomas, Commander F. F. E.,
106, *108*
'Young Guards', Russia, 190
Yugoslavia, 129–149

Zervas, General Napoleon,
154–158, *162*, 165–169
Zhukov, Marshal, 185
Zog I, King of Albania, 14, 15, 17,
18, 21
Zoliborz, Poland, 56
Zomer, 89

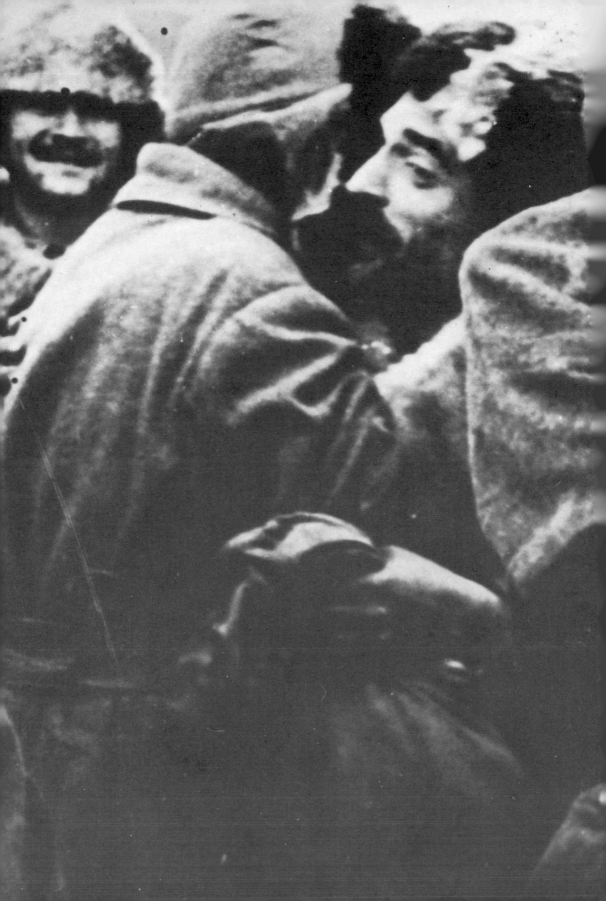